Who Has
Poisoned the Sea?

AUDREY COPPARD

Who Has
Poisoned the Sea?

MAMMOTH

First published in Great Britain 1970
by William Heinemann Ltd
Published 1992 by Mammoth
an imprint of Mandarin Paperbacks
Michelin House, 81 Fulham Road, London SW3 6RB

Mandarin is an imprint of the Octopus Publishing Group,
a division of Reed International Books Ltd

ISBN 0 7497 0266 4

A CIP catalogue record for this title
is available from the British Library

Typeset by Falcon Typographic Art Ltd,
Edinburgh & London
Printed in Great Britain
by Cox & Wyman Ltd, Reading, Berkshire

Contents

for
Greenpeace

1

Sunday at Home

Tim Dunwoodie looked round the door of his mother's bedroom for the seventh time that morning.

'When will lunch be ready?' he asked plaintively.

'Drat it, Tim, can't you forget your stomach for two minutes on end?' Her voice was muffled by a mouth full of pins. 'Can't you see how busy we are?'

Tess and Pauline were trying on pink brides-maid's dresses. Ellen was perched on the bed, busily sewing. His fourth sister, the bride-to-be, was being pinned into an ocean of white veil by his mother, who knelt in the foam of it, flustered and hot.

'Only three more weeks,' she sighed, 'and I'll never get half of it done in time.'

You will, Mum,' Ellen said soothingly. It was said as if the words had been repeated several times already that morning.

Tess was turning this way and that in front of the wardrobe mirror.

'Do you think it makes me look fat?'

'Yes,' Tim said, disgusted, and went downstairs again.

He looked in the fridge. Not even a piece of cheese or a fish finger. He counted the money in his pocket, and left the house.

It was only a short walk to the village sweet-shop. When he pushed open the door, a buzzer sounded, and Mrs Nelson appeared behind the counter.

'What'll you have? Quick!' she asked. 'I'm up to my elbows in pastry.'

The whole world seemed too busy that morning to spare him a moment. He looked down the High Street, sucking a toffee. Cars were streaming by, all in one direction. Normancote, where Tim lived, was on the main road, four miles inland from a resort on the coast. On fine Sunday mornings such as this, a thousand cars an hour rushed through the village and in the evening rushed back again. None of them ever stopped. Normancote did not have much to stop for. There was a cluster of houses round a nondescript church, and a small housing estate, where the Dunwoodies lived, which had been described by somebody in the local paper as an 'infernal eyesore'.

Tim's friend, Victor, came cycling up the street and waved. He waved back.

'Coming out this afternoon, Vic?'

'Can't. We've got people coming.'

'My place is like a madhouse. Everyone's trying on dresses.'

'What, for the wedding?'

'Yep. Lousy sisters.'

Victor made a rude noise in sympathy and cycled off.

Tim did not really feel gloomy. It was a sunny day, and there was still a week of the summer holidays left before he went back to school.

Better still, a lunch of sorts was being prepared when he got home again.

'You'll have to amuse yourself this afternoon,' his mother said. 'What will you do?'

'Oh, I'll go for a walk. Up on the hill, I think.'

He meant the high ridge behind the housing estate that led towards the sea.

His mother nodded, satisfied. The ridge was criss-crossed with footpaths used by ramblers and naturalists.

Tim often went off for walks on his own. Perhaps it was because he had so little privacy at home, but from an early age he had enjoyed exploring the countryside around his village. On one such walk, he had found a hollow, right at the top of a hill overlooking the sea. In the hollow there were wild flowers and butterflies, protected from the wind. A few small elder trees and bramble bushes grew around the rim, giving it a covered, secret air. And he called it his

Secret Dell and told no one about it except his grandfather.

The old man had been fixing a hook on his fishing rod when he mentioned the Dell.

'I found a hollow, right up on top of the hill there. It's got bushes growing round it.'

Grandfather looked up, interested. 'I know the place. They say that's where a plane crashed years ago.'

'A plane? You mean it made that big hole?'

'That's right. My brother remembered going up there to see the wreck.'

After that the Dell seemed even more special. Tim searched and searched but never found any sign of a plane, not even a little piece of metal.

On this particular Sunday, it was warm and quiet, with just the hum of insects and the wind rustling the bushes as it swept in from the sea. Tim picked some small blackberries which made his eyes water, they were so sour. Out at sea, great cloud shapes were massed in towers of grey and gold, driven by the rising wind, but in his Secret Dell it was warm and protected. Careful not to lie on a thistle, he lay stretched out and, without trying, soon fell asleep.

2

The Meeting with Edwin

Tim woke up with a start. A fly had landed on his ear and the humming had mingled with a dream all about planes flying low overhead, in from the sea, chasing each other. He scratched his ear and yawned. Once he had told his grandfather the Dell made him feel a little bit frightened because the pilot of the plane had died there.

'Don't be daft. England is so old, there can't be many places where someone or other hasn't died at some time. Take this cottage. Your grandma died here, and old Tom Tupper before her, and the Goodwins before that. But it ain't a bit creepy, is it?'

In the Dell it had suddenly turned very cold. Tim shivered and wished he had brought a jumper. The clouds were greyer and nearer now.

'Brr,' he said aloud to himself, 'it's freezing.'

Someone was watching him. He knew it, even

before he turned round. Someone was standing behind him, looking over the edge of the Dell.

He turned quickly and felt the hairs on the back of his neck rise with fear.

There was someone there. Someone with a bald head. On the pink scalp where hair should have been were blue, metallic looking knobs, shining faintly in the afternoon sun. And what made the sight really frightening was the fact that the bald head belonged to a young boy.

He was leaning over the edge of the hollow, staring fixedly at Tim, who sat, frozen with fear, at the bottom.

Because Tim had been thinking about the dead pilot, his first thought was that this was his ghost.

The stranger was wearing a short tunic of grey material, and long trousers and shoes all in one, like a pair of tights. And the strange, metallic shapes on his head.

If Tim had not been so frightened, he would have been aware that the other boy was just as frightened as he was.

He tried opening his mouth to shout or scream, but no sound came. There was silence for a full ten seconds, and then the boy spoke.

'I . . . I come in peace,' he said, his voice squeaking a little with nervousness. 'Where on earth am I?'

Tim still could not speak. His tongue was stuck to the roof of his mouth, but the boy's words had set his thoughts racing. This was no ghost. He was too young to be the ghost of the dead pilot and, anyway, he was far too real-looking. Tim's next thought was that the earth had been invaded from outer space. He certainly was a weird-looking boy, with those knobs on his head. And yet he had spoken in English, and had asked where on *earth* he was.

The boy in grey spoke again. 'Hairy one, where am I?'

Hairy one! Tim swallowed and found he was able to reply: 'Normancote. In K-Kent.'

The stranger frowned, and looked all about him. One of the attachments on his head glowed faintly. Then he turned and spoke again.

'That's strange. Normancote is where I am supposed to be. Yet everything looks so different.'

He started to walk down into the hollow, which made Tim huddle instinctively in a defensive way.

'Where is the College?'

Tim stared. 'There isn't a college. I mean, d-do you think you've got the right place?'

The boy snorted in a very human way, then shrugged. 'All I know is, I got off the airtrack at four o'clock to walk to the College in Normancote.' He held out his hands in a helpless gesture. 'I've got to get there right away for my history tests.'

Tim looked wildly about him at the bare hill. Then he had another, more frightening thought. Perhaps this was a madman, an escaped lunatic.

13

There was a big mental hospital not very far away. He had heard of one or two people escaping. Sometimes they could be quite dangerous.

As if he could sense Tim's new fears, the strange boy turned and gave a friendly smile.

'Please don't be frightened,' he said. 'Something very strange has happened. We must try to understand it.'

Tim nodded and gave a sickly grin. 'Yes,' he said brightly. 'Understand it.' If he was an escaped lunatic, the best thing to do was humour him.

'I was walking down the hill,' the boy was explaining, 'when one of my microcybs seemed to go wrong. I tried to mend it, knocked a wire off my telecyb, and then everything went cold and — different.'

'Well, yes, it would. Er, are those micro whatever you said?' Tim just had to ask, pointing at the knobs on the boy's head.

'Don't you know? Where's your set?'

Tim shook his head, and gave another sickly grin. Two of the knobs were glowing again faintly. The boy stood, considering Tim and the Dell.

'Tell me,' he suddenly said. 'What is the date?'

'Now I'm sure he's daft,' Tim thought, getting up on his feet ready to run. But he said the date, slowly and clearly, edging towards the other side of the hollow as he did so.

The boy in grey started to cry out as Tim told him, and his expression changed to one of horror.

14

'But this is awful! What has happened? When I walked down the road, it was the 28th of August, 2400.'

There was a shocked silence while they both considered this. Then the boy added, despairingly, 'Somehow I've projected myself backwards in time for four hundred years! Oh, drat these microcybs!'

3

Edwin

'Now whatever shall I do?' the boy said dejectedly.

Tim said nothing. His strongest wish at that moment was to run down the hill as fast as possible. He was shaking.

'Please don't run away.'

Tim jumped. The boy was looking at him strangely. But he stayed where he was.

'I think my telecyb is beginning to work. If you stay quiet, and try not to be frightened, I think we shall see into each other's minds.'

'All right,' Tim stammered, still sure the boy was mad.

'Shall we tell names?' he was asking, a little shyly. 'My name is Edwin.'

'Mine's Tim Dunwoodie.' In the silence that followed, he tried to master the panic that welled up inside him. He stopped shaking. Then a curious thing happened: the other boy's mind rose up and seemed to enter his own. All his fear melted away. Edwin was no longer a frightening stranger, a madman. He knew him. Their minds met and explored each other. He knew Edwin was kind, and frightened, and much more clever than he was. They stared at each other and sat down at the bottom of the Dell.

'So you are real? And not mad?'

'I thought the same of you!'

They both laughed, relief flooding them, making them want to talk.

'But how can you be here? I mean, these things you wear can't make it happen, can they?'

'Well, I've never heard of it happening before. It must have been a combination of things going wrong. But I can only draw tentative conclusions from insufficient data.'

Tim scratched his head, puzzled. 'Do you mean – guess?'

'Well, yes, I suppose so.' Edwin continued, 'All I know is what I have already told you. I was walking towards the College, across Campus Hill,' he gestured around him, 'and I stopped to adjust my history microcyb because it felt a bit loose. I knocked a wire out of my telecyb, and it must have got tangled up. Anyway, they're not working properly now.' He touched his head.

Tim sat, trying to believe this wonderful thing was really happening to him. Because he could see into his mind, he knew Edwin was telling him the truth. He could feel his curiosity, and wonder.

And right at the back of Edwin's mind, he could sense some pain, something large and deep.

'Edwin. That's a funny name. To me, that is.'

Edwin looked surprised. 'Is it? I thought it was an old English name.'

Tim could not disagree. 'Those things on your head, those knobs. They make you look – well, you look awful.'

He hoped he had not hurt Edwin's feelings, saying this, and was relieved to 'see' he had not.

'If your time doesn't have them and you've never seen them before, I am sure they do. I must say you look odd to me, with all that hair.'

Tim put out a finger, not quite daring to touch one of the microcybs. 'How do they work?'

'Do you know about computers?'

When Tim nodded, he went on, 'Ah, yes. They were just beginning in your time. Well, these are computers of a sort. It's more sensible to carry them around with you, and they work better when they are linked with human reasoning. It's a useful way to use their knowledge, that's all.'

'You said your history one had gone wrong. Does that mean you have a different one for different things?'

'Roughly. They have certain information in each, attached to the correct part of the brain by impulses, sort of electrical, do you understand? It's a bit complicated.'

Tim was sure of that. There were still a million

questions he wanted to ask, but his mind was too full of what he had already learned.

Now Edwin was asking a question. 'What are your clothes made of?'

Tim looked. 'Oh, all sorts. This is cotton. This is wool and nylon, I think.'

'Forgive me mentioning it, but they seem to absorb dirt.'

He looked down at his shorts and shirt. Certainly they could have been cleaner.

'What are yours made of, then?'

'Perfilx.' Edwin saw that the word was new to Tim and added, 'It has only been in use about twenty years. The material cleans itself by molecular vibration.'

'Oh. Anything else strange about me?'

Edwin considered for a moment. 'Nothing visual, except the hair. Surprisingly little, really.'

Then Tim thought of a new thing. 'If you've got telepathy knobs on your head, why do we have to talk?'

'I can't read your thoughts. Only your feelings, with a telecyb. It has no intellectual function.'

Tim struggled to understand. 'You mean, we can only tell things about each other, like, are we friendly towards each other, or are we frightened of each other?'

'Yes, that's it. But it does more. For instance, it shows up falsity.'

'I think I know what you mean. It's like a lie detector.'

'Except no one tells lies any more. There is no point.'

That was one use of telepathy that had never occurred to Tim. His head was swimming with excitement and all the fresh ideas.

'To think I thought you mad when we first met!'

Edwin nodded. 'Telecybs have helped people get over being mentally ill.'

Tim looked a little bewildered. 'I don't really understand everything you say, but you make the future sound a wonderful time.'

'We have solved some problems. We have others in their place . . .'

His voice trailed off with a sigh. Again Tim was aware of the pain at the back of Edwin's mind.

Edwin seemed to shrug off his troubles, whatever they were. 'But tell me about you,' he said. 'If I've gone back into history, I might as well use the time to mý own advantage and discover something from the mistake. If I get back to my own time, I'll know much more for my history examination if you tell me about life in Normancote about four hundred years ago.'

Tim looked doubtful. 'What sort of things do you want to know?'

'Well, let's start with you and your family. What sort of house you live in, what your parents do for a living, that sort of thing.'

Tim drew a deep breath. 'I don't know what Normancote is like in your time, but right now it's just a village. People do farming and work

20

in shops. There's a factory a few miles away. My father travels around the area, selling tractors and farm machinery. My mother works part-time in a shop.'

He stopped. He felt shy, he never liked talking about himself or his family. 'Is that the sort of thing?'

'Yes, yes. Do please go on. What about the rest of your family?'

'There's me and four sisters.'

Edwin looked surprised. 'What a big family! You are very lucky.'

'Lucky?' Tim practically choked. 'They're horrible! At least, Ellen isn't too bad, she's just a bit older than me. But the others – well, Vivienne, that's the oldest, she's getting married soon and you never saw such a fuss. All they do is talk about dresses and flowers and shoes until I could be sick. Pauline works in a hairdresser's, and Tess at a nursery. Not a baby nursery, a garden nursery.'

Edwin interrupted. 'Hairdressers? Women have their hair dressed?'

'I suppose women are bald in your time?' Tim thought that sounded horrible. He tried to imagine all his sisters bald.

'Anyway, that's us. We live down there.' He pointed towards the village. 'It's on a new housing estate, not very big.'

'What's the house made of?'

'Tiles, bricks, cement, you know, things like that.'

Edwin looked as surprised as if Tim had told him he lived in a cave.

'We've got electricity and television and telephones and things,' he finished off, a little lamely. He hoped Edwin wasn't going to ask him any really difficult questions about things like politics. To tell the truth, he was not even quite sure who the Prime Minister was, or how the Houses of Parliament worked. He knew the country was always being told to produce more and import less, but he never gave much thought to such matters. But Edwin seemed still to be thinking about the family.

'I wish I had a brother or a sister. Some people on the earth have two children, and in the space colonies they can have as many as they like, of course.'

'Space colonies? Do you mean people live on the stars?' Tim was almost shouting with excitement.

'Of course. Well, on planets, actually. But it isn't a very exciting life. The work is very dull and hard, only people like geologists and miners go to live there.'

'And what about people from outer space?' Tim could hardly bring himself to ask. 'Are there any in outer space?'

'None that I know of. So far as we know, we are the only people in the universe.' He laughed. 'Don't look so disappointed!'

They talked together for a long while, asking

each other questions, putting forward ideas. Tim told Edwin about cars and rockets and comics, about his school, and about money.

'I can't imagine how this will help you with your history exam,' he finished up.

'It will, though. This is the sort of social history I need.'

'Social history? What's that?'

'Microcybs tell of things like wars and kings and queens and trade, but they don't tell what kind of television programmes people watched, or how many children are in a class.'

'I'm on holiday from school still. But we go back next week.' Tim paused. It seemed ridiculous to be saying 'next week' to somebody who lived over four hundred years from now.

Edwin was thinking of something else, and spoke in a dreamy way. 'This is a sort of miracle, isn't it? More than a dream. It is quite outside anything we both know as normal, and yet we have to accept it.'

'It's like a dream to me. I keep feeling as if I'm going to wake up.'

'In some ways I wish it were a dream. Then I would not have to worry about getting back to my own time.'

Edwin made an expressive gesture that Tim thought very beautiful and graceful. He never used his own hands like that.

'But while I am still here, let's talk some more about you. You were saying you are on holiday?'

'Yes. We've just come back from two weeks in Cornwall.'

'Cornwall? By the sea?' Tim noticed that Edwin sounded a little bit strange. 'What did you do there?'

'The usual. I've got a new fishing rod, and Dad and I did some fishing. We swam and went on a boat. Picnicked on the beach. You know.'

Edwin was not looking at him. The pain that Tim had sensed at the back of all they said to each other suddenly flared up in the boy's brain, and hit him as if the pain were a blow.

Edwin spoke, almost mumbled. 'We can't do those things now, in my time. We can no longer go swimming, or fish, or even walk on the beach. The sea is a terrible, horrible place and we dare not go near. In my time, the sea has been poisoned.'

4

The Poisoned Sea

'Poisoned? The whole sea?' Tim was shaken and unbelieving. 'You can't poison a whole sea!'

Edwin nodded sorrowfully, helplessly. 'You can, or someone can. Someone has. Well, nearly all. And it's spreading. We don't know what the poison is, that's the terrible thing about it. All we know is it starts in the middle of the Atlantic, and it is new, and quite deadly.'

Tim looked at his friend's unhappy face. He was shaken by the strength of his pain. 'That is what is making you so sad. I could feel it all along,' he said gently.

'Yes.'

They sat quietly together, and Tim waited for Edwin to go on. As if it could hold the answer, they both turned to look out to sea. It was no longer sparkling, but looked grey and heavy under the advancing clouds.

'It did not start too long ago. Only about five

years. Up until then, the sea was just like it's always been. At first the scientists thought it was atomic waste. That still crops up from time to time. Then they thought it was coming up from inside the earth itself. But it wasn't. They got more and more frightened, because it seemed to be some sort of chain reaction, constantly growing. It can't be stopped. It kills the fish, and every form of life in the sea wherever it goes.'

The pain seared and burned. Tim could hardly bear it.

Edwin went on in the same flat tone. 'My family also live near the sea. Like most people who can, we own a pet dolphin. I've had mine since I was five. He's part of the family . . .'

Tim hardly dared ask. 'Is he dead?'

'No. He lives in a tank in our garden now. But he is very sick, the poison has got into him. And as no one knows what it is, we can't make him well. And he pines for the sea and his friends. He will certainly die.'

So that was it. That was the desperate sorrow that Edwin could not hide. Once Tim had owned a guinea-pig and it had died. He had cried about it, but knew he had felt nothing like the pain and love that Edwin felt for his dolphin.

'Do you think your scientists will find out soon?'

'They are working on it, day and night,' Edwin replied in a steadier voice. 'It's not just the fish and the dolphins. You see, the poison is spreading to places where people rely on fish for their food. There is a lot of ocean-bed farming. All that will have to stop, and thousands of people may starve.'

The part that seemed most real to Tim was the dolphin.

Edwin was trying to smile. 'I can't remember if you have pet dolphins in your time.'

'No, not really. I've heard of places where they are trained to play with balls and do tricks.'

'It's coming soon, then. They really are very intelligent, you know. Much more than other animals.'

'What can they do?'

'Heaps of things. They can take messages to the ocean-bed farms. They mend damaged cables. They tell us where to find the most fish. Apart from being such fun. My dolphin, he's called Beppo, taught me to swim and dive and love the sea.'

'That's his name, then, Beppo.' Tim tried to express his sympathy. 'You make him sound such fun. I've got a snorkel and flippers.'

'Oh, we can do better than that!' Edwin laughed. 'We have a gas now, in my time, that when you inhale it, your lungs fill up with solid oxygen, so you can stay under the water, and dive deep . . .'

Both boys were growing tired with the effort to understand each other's different worlds. They were silent for a while. Then Edwin spoke again about his pet dolphin.

27

'Beppo can't talk, but we understand each other. He has taught me some of the movements dolphins use for language. And lately, some of the cleverest ones, like Beppo, have taken to wearing telecybs.'

'Those knobs!' Tim spluttered.

'They do look funny! Especially the ones that carry satchels.'

'Satchels?'

'They carry them when they take messages under the sea.'

It was too much for Tim: dolphins wearing satchels and knobs on their heads. 'I don't believe it.'

'It's true! And listen, did you know that dolphins dance? Beppo took me on his back one day to watch it for myself. Right out at sea. It was a ritual dance, something to do with their language.'

'I might believe it if I saw it.'

'I don't think you ever will. At least, I think you live too long ago.'

'It's hard enough believing in *you*.'

'I know.'

'I mean, although you wear telecybs and things, you aren't all that much different from me, are you?'

Edwin shook his head. 'But the world has gone through a lot between your time and mine. We have had to make life a lot simpler, much more like it used to be, otherwise there probably would be no people left at all. I don't think I should tell you all about it. I think somehow I shouldn't tell you too much. But we are living in what is known as the Age of Simplification.'

'Oh. But do all the people wear microcybs? Or just some?'

'Most people. There are a few who do not. They are the ones we call Elders. They do not wear them because they no longer need to. No one can be quite sure why, or what has happened to their brains, but they are changing into a new type of human being. It's nothing to be frightened of, though. Probably it is the way all human minds will go in a few hundred years. They can read each other's minds without telecybs. In lots of ways they are different.'

'Can't they tell you what poisoned the sea?'

'Not yet. I suppose if anyone can find out what it is, they will.'

'Are they your leaders?'

'No. They are just ordinary men and women to begin with, and when they find out their brains are developing, they go to live together, very simply. Anyone can ask their advice if they want to, of course.'

'I wish I could help find out about the poison.'

'Some scientists think it may have started about your time. They think it has taken a long time to change into what it is. I just don't know.'

They sat, quietly, comfortably, like old friends. It could not last. Already Edwin was thinking about how to return. He looked at the sky.

The sun had shifted and now was hidden by the banking clouds. It was late afternoon.

'Well, it looks as if I have missed the examinations,' Edwin sighed. 'Whatever shall I use as an excuse?'

Tim said nothing. He was thinking it would be hard for Edwin to get back to his own time to make any kind of excuse at all. He looked at the microcybs.

'When you do go, Edwin, I don't suppose we shall ever meet again.'

They both felt sad. 'It isn't likely.' Edwin gave one of his beautiful gestures. 'I came by a series of errors, and I think it would be impossible to repeat them. But what worries me is how to reverse the process, and go back.'

Tim realized suddenly how brave Edwin was being.

'Do you know, if it had been me, I would have just sat screaming for help. I wouldn't have asked lots of questions like you have.'

'That's not true. I can tell that, given half a chance, you would come back to my time with me.' Edwin smiled kindly. 'And that shows you're braver than you think.'

It was true. Tim realized that, for quite a time, he had been thinking how marvellous it would be to enter Edwin's world for a little while, just as the boy had entered his.

Edwin was trying to untwist one of the telecybs on his head.

Tim watched, then said, 'When our television set goes wrong, a good bash on the side always gets it going again. At least, that's what my dad always does, and it seems to work.'

Edwin was laughing at him. 'No wonder you are known to us as the Age of Amateurs! Somehow I don't think that kind of behaviour works with microcybs.'

Tim felt hurt. At once Edwin reacted to his mood.

'All the same, I'll try it. No harm done if I give them a little shake.'

He did so, and laughed at Tim again, 'There, I . . .' He was gone. Tim could see nothing of him. The Dell, the hill, the sky, everything was as it had been before, except he was now on his own. The air suddenly felt warmer than before, full of a clammy heat. From out at sea, he heard the rumble of thunder.

Tim got shakily to his feet, and looked about him, just to make sure Edwin was not there.

Then he stumbled down the hill towards his home.

5

The Storm

'You look pale as a ghost.' It was Ellen who first noticed Tim. He was standing just inside the kitchen, leaning against the wall. His eyes looked black and large with delayed shock. He tried to speak, but no words would come out properly.

'I . . . I . . .' he stammered.

Ellen put an arm round her young brother and began to look really concerned.

'What's wrong?'

He allowed himself to be led across to a chair, and the familiar, warm smell of the kitchen, with its ticking clock and his family all about, helped to calm him.

'Whatever's wrong?' His mother bent over him, feeling his forehead as she did so. It felt clammy and cold. 'Have you seen an accident?'

He shook his head and gave a short, rather hysterical giggle.

'No, a ghost more likely.'

He had the attention of all of them now. 'What's he talking about?' they asked excitedly. 'Where, what happened?'

He looked round. Ellen still looked worried for his sake, his mother still bent over him, Pauline and Tess were staring at him with their mouths open.

'I've been up on the top of the hill, at the Dell.'

'What Dell?'

He shook his head, as if denying what he had just said. 'No, it's a mistake. I didn't see anything.'

'Oh, come on, Tim. You must have seen something to look so queer. What was it?'

He shook his head again and set his lips firmly in a tight line. He could not tell them. The meeting with Edwin could not be put into easy words. Perhaps if his mother had been on her own he could have explained, or perhaps he could have told Ellen. But the others, who had teased him all his life, scoffed at everything he did, they could not be trusted with this story. He knew just what they would say, and how they would laugh.

He huddled down in the chair and closed his eyes.

There was a long drawn out rumbling that drew their attention away from him. They looked up at the darkening window.

'Storm's coming,' his mother said, going to the door.

The storm certainly was coming. The sky was a dull, leaden grey pressing close to the earth, and a sudden flurry of wind caught at the trees. Pauline switched on the lights and then dashed upstairs to close the windows against the rain.

Ellen looked at Tim in a questioning sort of way, but she said nothing. He gave her a wobbly grin, and escaped to his room.

From his window, he watched the storm. Time passed, but no one came to disturb him. He must have stood there, motionless, for an hour. Then, with the coming of night, the lightning and thunder passed a long way away. There was just an occasional twitch of lightning, and soon nothing at all.

A figure quietly entered the room and Tim, whose nerves were in such a torn state, gave a jump and a gasp of fright. But it was only Ellen, looking strange in the dim half-light.

'It's me.'

They stood companionably together at the window, while Ellen brushed her long, black hair. Tim listened to the quiet noise she made: swish, swish.

'I did see something,' he said.

'I thought so.'

'It's just that I couldn't say in front of the others.'

Ellen nodded. He just managed to see it in the nearly dark room.

'There was this boy, about my age, up on the

34

hill. He looked very strange. You could tell he was from the future.'

Ellen drew in her breath. 'How?'

'It went very cold, and then he just appeared. I was scared, but he was too.'

'Did he speak?'

'Oh, yes. We talked for a long time. I know you won't believe me.'

Ellen's brush was now still. 'Go on,' was all she could say.

'I can hardly believe it myself, now. At first I was so scared, I thought he was a lunatic. Then we talked and we got to be friends. I don't know how it happened exactly. At least I do, but it's hard to put into words. He was wearing microcybs and they went wrong, so it was all an accident really.'

Ellen held his hand tight.

'Did he do anything?'

'Do anything? No, we just talked. I told you, we just told each other about everything, and got to be friends.'

There was a strange note in Tim's voice that Ellen did not like or understand. She could feel him trembling when she touched him.

'Do you mind if I call Mum?' she asked, her own voice not very steady either.

'No, you can get her now. I don't mind talking about it.'

'And do you mind if I turn on the light?'

'OK.'

She hurried downstairs. Tim slowly got into his pyjamas and waited for them to come. Whatever they made of it, just telling the story would be a relief. The only trouble was, the whole thing sounded less likely every time he thought about it.

His mother came in and sat on the bed, Ellen beside her. Obviously she had heard something of what had happened already, because her normally pink face was very pale, and she looked at her son with great concern.

'Now, you just tell me exactly what happened.'

He tried to look and sound normal. 'I saw a sort of apparition. I mean, he wasn't a ghost and he looked real enough, but he told me he was from the future.'

'Did he hurt you?'

'No.'

'Ellen said you talked. What did he tell you, what did he say?'

'It was mostly about how life was then, and he wanted to know about mine. He said he lived four hundred years from now. He was wearing sort of computers on his head, and one of them was for making us telepathic. It was something going wrong with the computers that sent him back in time.'

He stopped. There was no way of knowing how his mother would take such a story.

'It was someone pulling your leg.'

'No.' The one word hung in the air between them, full of conviction.

His mother shook her head in a helpless sort of way. 'I don't say it's impossible. I mean, I do believe in telepathy. I think it runs in the family too. I've had twinges myself, but this is . . .'

Ellen put in gently, 'Tim couldn't have made up such a story could he, Mum? And we don't know what inventions they will have in the future. And this boy said it was an accident.'

Tim listened to them, as he lay twisting at a corner of his blanket. 'But Mum, that isn't all he told me. He told me a dreadful thing, something that is going to happen. He said the sea was poisoned in his time, and it was spreading, and all the fish were being killed.'

'Good God, did he say what it was?'

'They didn't know. It might come from something dumped in the sea. And their scientists are all working on it, to try and stop it, and some of them think it has taken hundreds of years to happen.'

'We are poisoning it already,' Mrs Dunwoodie said sharply. She spoke as someone who had supported the Green Party for years. 'All this atomic waste, and oil and I don't know what else.'

Tim shook his head. 'No, it's none of them. It must be something else, something that doesn't seem likely to poison anything. Edwin said it was a completely new kind of poison.'

'Edwin?'

'That was his name.'

Ellen giggled. 'Poor chap, fancy being called Edwin.'

Mrs Dunwoodie sat thinking it all over. Tim felt wonderfully comforted to see she actually believed the story. Everything seemed more normal, and gradually he stopped trembling.

'I wish your dad was here.'

'So do I.'

'I don't think it's a story to throw around, though.'

Tim agreed with her. 'Please don't tell the others, Mum,' he begged.

'The only people who ought to know are the scientists. Or someone in the know. They might be able to work it all out and make more sense of it than I can. Oh, I get *so* angry, when I think of all that pollution . . .' His mother cared deeply about what she said was all about money and nobody caring for nature.

'But who could I tell? We don't know any scientists.' Tim thought about it, and wondered what scientists would say. Would they try and help solve the riddle of the poison, or would they laugh and tell him not to be so silly?

'Perhaps Grandad can help,' Ellen said.

'Yes, now that *is* a good idea,' Mrs Dunwoodie agreed. 'He worked at those laboratories at Shenton for years as caretaker. He must have got to know a few scientists.'

'Even if they do laugh at me, I'm going to try and save Beppo.'

Ellen creased her forehead. 'Beppo? You said his name was Edwin.'

'No, Edwin's the boy. Beppo is his dolphin.'

'Dolphin? You didn't say anything about dolphins.'

And so, of course, Tim had to tell them the whole story again, this time leaving out nothing, and before his tale was finished the church clock struck eleven times. Then Ellen went downstairs to make some cocoa, but before she returned, Tim had fallen asleep on his bed. She tucked him in, turned out the light, and silently shut the door.

6

Grandfather

When Tim woke up the next morning, he could feel it was late. He heard church bells. Remembrance of what had happened the day before suddenly flooded in on him. He lay still, thinking and thinking about it, trying to sort out in his mind what had been said, what had been felt, and the tremendous responsibility of it all.

'How can I save Beppo?' he thought, almost with terror. 'Why should this happen to me?'

The answer to that, he knew, was not important. It *had* happened, and out of all the millions of people in England, he was the one involved. It was a very lonely feeling.

Perhaps because he had so much on his mind, or perhaps because he had gone to bed much too late, Tim found himself snapping at everyone and being so unreasonable that he was soon left alone by the rest of the family.

In the afternoon, his mother said, 'You're like

a bear with a sore head. If you can't control your temper you'd better go out. Here, take these clean clothes over to your grandfather's for me. And try and stop scowling.'

He said he was too tired, and it was too wet, but in the end he wheeled his bicycle out of the shed and pedalled the mile to his grandfather's cottage. It was a sodden day; the gutters were gurgling, and wet leaves whirled up in the cold wind. Grandfather was in. He did not look very pleased to see Tim, perhaps because he had been asleep. But his temper improved when he found half an ounce of tobacco tucked into one of his clean socks. He put the kettle on, and got down two mugs and the biscuit tin from the kitchen dresser. Tim took a custard cream. Grandfather spooned sugar into their cups and stirred the tea. Then he put his false teeth in and took two biscuits.

'What's the matter with you this afternoon? Cat got your tongue?'

'There's nothing wrong with me,' Tim snapped back.

Grandfather snorted. 'Glad to come over here and escape all those sisters?'

There was a not very good-natured silence for a minute or two, and then Tim said, 'You know that place up on the hill, where the plane crashed?'

'You know I know. It was me told you about it.'

'I went there yesterday.'

41

The old man just looked at him. There was another silence.

'All right. So you went there. What am I supposed to say?'

Tim decided his grandfather could be a nasty, old, bad tempered man at times. He waited until his grandfather's pipe was drawing nicely, then tried again.

'I saw someone there.'

This time his grandfather did not even bother to reply.

'He – this person I saw – said he was from the future.'

'And I'm the Queen of Sheba.'

Tim stood up. 'If you're going to be like that, I just won't bother to tell you.'

Something in the boy's strained, white face stopped Grandfather from snapping back.

'Sit down, for goodness sake. No need to get shirty.'

'Will you listen to me, then?'

'Talk sense, and I'll listen.'

Satisfied, Tim sat down again.

'Don't ask me how it happened, but this boy . . .'

'Boy?'

'. . . yes, boy about my age – he just appeared from nowhere and he looked funny and different and at first I thought he was an escaped lunatic. You know, from the hospital up the way.'

'And was he? What made him look funny?'

'I don't mean *funny*. He was wearing things on his head, wiry things with knobs that looked like blue glass. He said they were little computers.'

'Well. I've heard of some leg pulls in my time.'

'It wasn't!' Tim almost shouted. 'I would have known if it was! He got into telepathic communication with me, because they can do that sort of thing, in the future.'

For the first time, Grandfather looked as though he might believe the story. 'Well, that runs in the family, telepathy. Did I ever tell you about the time . . .'

Tim interrupted, 'That's what Mum said.'

'Ah, you've told her, then?'

Tim nodded. 'She doesn't know what to make of it.'

'I'm not surprised. Her son goes off for a walk and comes back and says he's been in touch with the future and talked to some bloke with knobs on.'

'I didn't say she didn't believe me! She does. But she says I ought to see a scientist or someone who knows more about things. Because this boy, he was called Edwin, told me something awful that might start happening in our time and poison the sea.'

The old man was sitting up straight in his chair now, his cup of tea growing cold. It was impossible to watch Tim's sincere and desperate face without believing that something had happened

43

to the boy. Even if it turned out to be a hoax, or a dream, he had to take it seriously for Tim's sake.

'I know a few scientists,' he said. 'Don't know if they'll help, mind, but I got quite chummy with one or two of them. What's all this about poisoning the sea?'

So Tim told him the whole story and at the end of it, found he was crying with nerves. Grandfather quietly handed him a handkerchief and tactfully went away to make some more tea.

'You all right?' he asked when he came back.

'Yes thanks,' Tim sniffed.

'Well, that's the rummest story I ever heard. I don't say I don't believe it. I know you couldn't have made it up if you tried. But it takes a bit of swallowing for all that.'

'Do you think anyone will believe me?'

'Well, your mum does for a start, and Ellen you say, and I suppose I do. And,' he added surprisingly, 'your sister knows a lot about pollution.'

'You mean Ellen?'

'You ask her about it. Last time she came here, she told me about the things they are doing at school. Recycling paper, cleaning up waste ground, planting trees. And the pupils write to the papers and the local council if something goes wrong. The school made a fuss when some factory or other poured chemicals into the sea. You ask her.'

Tim thought about it. He wasn't surprised – Ellen had been a vegetarian for years. She said she couldn't bear to think of eating animals that had been locked up just so that her meat and eggs were cheaper. But Tim was not very interested and hadn't listened to what she said.

'I think about the dolphins all the time now, Grandad. I don't worry about chickens and pigs like Ellen does. Perhaps I should.'

'I don't know about that,' Grandad said practically. 'But just now it looks like you've got a crisis on your hands. We'll do what we can. I'll see if this scientist I know at Grand Universal will help.'

'Tell a stranger? I can't! They'll laugh!'

'Maybe, maybe not. But you've got to start somewhere; unless you want to drop it now.'

'I meant it when I said I'd do anything to save that Beppo. But you won't make it into a joke, will you, Grandad? You won't make fun of it?'

'Tell him yourself if you think I'm not up to it', the old man replied gruffly.

'I don't want people to laugh, that's all.'

'We don't know he'll even see us yet. And we don't need to say much. Just about the poison and that. Ask about anything new that's being dumped in the sea, that sort of thing.' He pointed towards his newspaper. 'I spend a lot of time these days reading the paper. I can tell you, some of the things going on are terrible. There was a story last week about seals being washed up on the coast, dead from pollution, they think. And there was talk of nerve gas escaping in the Irish Sea . . .'

45

'Will he know about chemicals in the sea, your scientist?'

'Sure to. Now, you get off home, and thank your mum for the tobacco.'

He went, and all the way home, Tim rehearsed in his mind what he would say to the strange scientist. It was no use – the story seemed much too fantastic to convince a stranger and a scientist. Didn't they always like proof?

But his grandfather's offer to help had cheered him up, and he no longer felt he carried all the weight of it on his own. When he got home, his mother was pleased to see him smiling and calm once again.

7

Grand Universal Laboratories

There was not much industry in that part of Kent, and Grand Universal Laboratories was the biggest employer of local men and women in the district. Of course, Grand Universal had factories all over England, but the one at Shenton employed scientists working on research into plastics and food. And a number of things that the laboratories were involved in were top secret.

The scientist Grandfather was going to meet shared a hobby with the older man: a passion for fishing. They had first met on one of the quiet backwaters in the area, and competed with each other to get the best fish. After that, they would often meet both at work and on the river banks, and talk about the state of the rivers, and where the best fish were to be found; but all Grandfather knew about him was that his name was Crossfield and he was the head of one of Grand Universal's synthesizing departments.

'Dunwoodie? I wonder what he wants with me?' Crossfield frowned when he heard who was on the phone. Then his bushy, sandy eyebrows shot up in surprise when he heard the old man wanted to come and see him, and bring his grandson. He wondered if the boy was interested in becoming a scientist, but he seemed a bit young to be deciding that.

'Could you both be here about 4.30 then?' he asked, looking at his diary. 'I'll meet you downstairs if you ask for me.'

Grandfather then telephoned Tim. 'Wear a clean shirt whatever you do,' he ordered, 'and meet me in time for the ten-to-four bus.'

'Why? Where are we going?'

'Grand Universal, of course,' said Grandfather, very importantly, and hung up.

Tim was very nervous. He cleaned his shoes and borrowed one of his father's nice, big handkerchiefs. His mother gave him a vague kiss when it was time to go.

'Can't see it will do any harm, talking to this man. But don't expect too much from him, love.'

'But it was you who suggested it!'

'Did I?'

It was obvious she had too many other things on her mind, and Tim felt let down. But he was wrong. She was looking in her handbag, and fished out a sheet of paper. 'I made a list of people who might help, that's if this scientist

48

friend of your grandfather's is no good. There's Greenpeace, Save the Whales, Friends of the Earth . . .'

Ellen came into the kitchen just then and asked what was going on.

'Tim and Grandfather are going to Grand Universal to see a scientist.'

Ellen looked impressed.

'Last time I saw Grandad, he said *you* know a lot about the environment,' Tim said.

'Well, we have this club at school, "Save Our Planet" it's called. Of course we get called the SOPpies, but we don't mind. It's really interesting. Don't you have something like that at your school?'

'I don't think so,' said Tim, not sure. He remembered seeing posters on the noticeboard about saving the whales and the greenhouse effect, and asking them not to throw things away. It was all very complicated, but perhaps there was a connection with Beppo and what the posters said. 'Perhaps I should ask this scientist about what gets dumped in the sea.'

'No, Tim,' his mother said in her Stand No Nonsense voice. 'You just stick to your story, that will be quite enough.'

Walking down the hill to the bus stop, Tim suddenly panicked. Again he thought, 'Why me? Why should I get mixed up in this? Why not just forget all about it?' But he knew he could not. He would never be able to forget the way

Edwin had looked when he told him about the poisoned sea and about Beppo. Then, because he was thinking so hard about Beppo, he walked straight into a tree.

'Ouch!' He had hurt his knee, and he bent to rub it. A strange dizziness came over him, and there was a buzzing in his ears. From far off, or near – he could not tell from where – he heard a voice, calling his name.

'Tim! Tim!' it whispered (shouted?).

He looked all around him, but there was no one there. A cold wind stirred the trees and a wet leaf fell on his face. It made him jump.

'Tim!' the voice called again, and suddenly he was sure it was the voice of Edwin.

'Edwin!' he shouted wildly. 'Where are you?'

Then he heard the voice again, this time quite clearly, saying a name he did not know. 'Tim! It's Tribaxin . . . TRIBAXIN. Can you hear?'

'Yes; yes! Where are you? Edwin!'

But all was still. The dizzy feeling cleared from his head, and he strained his ears for some new sound. But none came.

With a last look about him, he turned and ran down the hill to the bus stop. The strange word kept ringing in his head: Tribaxin. What did it mean?

Grandfather was already at the bus stop. Tim rushed up and started to tell him what had happened, but the old man cut him short.

'You look a scarecrow! And what have you done to your knee?'

He himself was wearing his best blue suit, and his white moustache was newly trimmed. He looked very nice and very excited.

But Tim's attention was not on clothes. He sniffed and then held his nose. 'Hey, what's that awful smell?'

There was a bundle of newspaper under Grandfather's arm from where the smell seemed to emanate.

'If you must know, it's a fish for Mr Crossfield.'

'A fish?'

'Yes. A trout I caught up near Paddock.' He was chuckling to himself. 'He'll be green with envy when he sees it.'

'Smells as if the fish is green, more like.'

He got a friendly cuff on the ear for that, and then the bus came, so he did not have a chance to tell Grandfather about the strange voice and the word that had been whispered so urgently.

They sat down in the front, and then Tim started to feel nervous all over again. His stomach hurt and he wanted to go back home.

'Is he nice?'

'What, Mr Crossfield? Seems decent enough. Goes fishing with me now and then. Not much good, though.' He started to chuckle again and squeezed his fishy bundle tighter. Tim said nothing. He guessed that Mr Crossfield was a very good angler indeed, and that was why Grandfather was going to so much trouble to impress him.

'If Mr Crossfield goes fishing, he's bound to know a lot about pollution, isn't he?'

Grandfather agreed. 'One of the worst patches is up by Telby's farm — a whole lot of fertilizer ran into the stream. Killed all the fish.'

'So perhaps he'll understand — about how awful Edwin feels . . .'

'Grandfather cut him short. 'This is where we get off.'

Grand Universal Laboratories was set back from the main road and had a floral clock in front of it. There was also a large car park, and Tim stopped to look at some of the cars.

'Look at that Italian sports! Does it belong to one of the scientists?'

'More likely one of the managers.'

Grandfather was pulling him on towards the front door, very confident and brisk, now he was back in his familiar work ground again. The entrance hall was bright with flowers, and very large. There were black leather armchairs scattered about. Behind a glass desk sat a receptionist, who welcomed them with a lovely smile.

'Mr Dunwoodie? It is nice to see you again.'

Grandfather took off his hat and fingered his moustache.

'You're looking lovelier than ever, Miss Evelyn. I've come to see Mr Crossfield — I think he expects me.'

They sank down into two armchairs while the

receptionist talked into the telephone on her desk. Tim looked about. It was nothing like he had imagined a laboratory to be. He had expected a sort of hospital smell, and people in white coats everywhere. All he could see, whenever a door opened off the entrance hall, were offices.

The receptionist flashed her smile. 'You're to go down to the canteen. Mr Crossfield will meet you at the lift.'

They walked down a flight of steps, and a man with sandy eyebrows was waiting for them.

'Mr Crossfield.'

'Mr Dunwoodie.' They all shook hands, and Tim was introduced.

'Would you like some tea? It's easier to have a chat in the canteen. I've got a lot on upstairs today; there's a bit of a crisis, and we might have been interrupted.'

'I know how busy you are. What we've got to say won't take too long.'

'I didn't mean to hurry . . .' Mr Crossfield crinkled up his eyes when he smiled; and Tim suddenly decided he liked him. He was not sure how old he was, but he looked younger than his own father. About thirty, he guessed.

They went along the counter with their trays, and Mr Crossfield piled cakes on a plate. 'Come on, take one of those doughnuts. How about some biscuits? Take two. Orange to drink? Or tea?'

Tim was too shy to say anything, but soon

sat down with a large plate of food in front of him.

Grandfather cleared his throat and looked at Mr Crossfield intently.

'Now for it,' Tim thought. 'He's going to tell him now.'

But he did not. 'Have a look in this parcel,' he said, 'I think it might interest you.'

Mr Crossfield unwrapped the newspaper to reveal a large, silvery trout. His eyebrows shot up in surprise.

'What a whopper! Where did you land it?'

Grandfather looked triumphant. 'You know that little stretch past Paddock? Where you said there weren't any trout to be had?'

Mr Crossfield looked disbelieving. 'Never.'

'True as I sit here.'

They all looked at the fish again. It really was beginning to smell strongly. Mr Crossfield wrapped it up in the newspaper again and pushed it back to Grandfather.

'No, no, I don't want it back. I meant it for you, it's a little present.'

'That is kind.' Mr Crossfield smiled, but Tim noticed he pushed the parcel as far away up the table as he could.

'Is that what you came to see me about?'

Now was the moment. Tim waited, crossing his fingers under the table.

'No. My grandson here would like some advice, and I couldn't think of a better person to come to.'

'Only too glad to help, if I can.'

'It's in your line, I think.'

'My line?' Mr Crossfield scratched his sandy hair, and looked at Tim. 'Do you mean food synthesis?'

'I don't know what that is.' He chose his words with care. 'What I wanted to find out about was to do with poisons. Things that could poison the sea.'

'Ah. You've come to the right man, then. Not so much because of my work, but because of my hobby.'

'You mean fishing?'

'Right. There's nothing I'd like better than to see the rivers pure again, and see some more fish in them.'

'Then you would know what kinds of things poison the sea?'

'All of it? That's a lot of water. I can think of lots of things that might do a bit of local poisoning, but not the whole sea.'

'Could you give me a list? Things like oil and detergents?'

'Is this for some kind of school test?'

Tim did not answer but Grandfather cut in. 'He's doing a sort of project. Here you are, here's a bit of paper.'

He produced an old, torn envelope and a stubby pencil. 'Here, write your list on there.'

Mr Crossfield smiled. 'Hold on a minute. It's not that simple, you know. Give me time to think.

It doesn't have to be a poison to start with. It's a question of the balance of nature. All sorts of things can act like a poison, put in the wrong place. For instance, a bit of fertilizer on the land is fine, but too much in the water, and the wrong things grow. The oxygen gets used up, and then a lot of marine life can be poisoned.'

'That's just what I was saying, wasn't it, Tim?'

Mr Crossfield wrote some words down and passed the paper to Tim.

'It's a short list, but I don't think I've left anything out. There's atomic waste and any amount of chemicals, and oil, of course. And sewage. And there are metallic wastes, oh, and . . .' He busily wrote a list of names that Tim found impossible to read upside down.

'Thank you very much.'

'I'm afraid the list gets longer with time. So many things are dumped in the sea, and some of them are bound to turn out poisonous in the long run.'

There was one more thing Tim wanted to know.

'Please, Sir, have you heard of Tribaxin?'

Mr Crossfield's eyebrows wobbled again. 'Tribaxin! How did you hear about that?'

'I don't know,' Tim floundered.

'It's very new – very hush-hush.' The scientist looked a bit cross that Tim had heard of it.

'Do you mind telling me what we're all talking about?' Grandfather demanded.

Mr Crossfield looked over his shoulder, and then leaned forward so that he could speak in a low voice.

'It's a brand new plastic. Hardly in production yet, and made by some of our boys. When it does come on the market, it's likely to put all the others out of business.'

'What makes it so special?'

'Ah, that's the secret bit. It has a different structure, different melting point, the lot. You can make anything out of it.'

Tim was dying to know more. His heart was pounding with excitement at this new discovery. So the word did mean something! The voice had been a warning, telling him to do something about Tribaxin, of that he felt sure.

'Is Tribaxin one of the new plastics that doesn't last for ever, what's the word . . .'

Mr Crossfield helped him out. 'Biodegradable? Yes, I believe it is.'

Grandfather was looking at Tim curiously. 'You never told me about this whatsit. Where did you hear about it?'

'I must have heard someone talking about it on the bus or somewhere.'

The two men seemed satisfied with this explanation.

'Have I helped your project?'

'Oh, yes. Thanks a lot.' They all stood up. 'And thanks for the lovely tea.' Mr Crossfield picked up his fish.

'Does your grandson do any fishing?'

'He drops a hook in the water now and then.'

'Perhaps we'll meet up one day, then,' he said, 'and perhaps we'll find this trout's brother.'

The three of them left the building, and the receptionist waved good-bye.

'Come again, if you want to,' Mr Crossfield said to Tim.

'Thanks. I will,' he promised.

Back home again, Tim pulled the list out of his pocket and studied it. Somehow, he did not believe the things on the list had anything to do with Edwin's poisoned sea. Not any more. Everything on it was so obvious – the scientists in Edwin's time would have thought of them all. So it was more likely to be something different, something that nobody would think of. Something like plastic.

He lay on his bed, thinking. Knowing about this Tribaxin was one thing. Knowing what to do next was a bit more difficult. He would talk to Ellen. She knew more about saving the whales and the rain forests and things like that. And she was even more soft-hearted than he was. Ellen would understand how much it meant to him to try to save Beppo. She would care too that things going wrong now might destroy him in four hundred years' time.

8

The Wedding

The holidays were over, and it was time for Tim to go back to school. There was so much to think about that he pushed the problems of Edwin, Beppo and Tribaxin to the back of his mind.

It was Ellen who brought the matter up again one day, when their mother was not yet home from work and they were alone in the kitchen after school.

'That boy, Edwin, I suppose he knew a terrific lot.'

'Mmm.' Tim answered through a mouthful of toast. 'He did, although there were lots of things he wouldn't tell me. But I suppose there would be more to know in four hundred years' time, anyway.'

'How do you mean?'

'Take us. We know more than they did even a hundred years ago, when there weren't any cars, or aeroplanes or television. Think of all the inventions there must have been between our time and Edwin's.'

Ellen thought about it. 'And yet he didn't sound so different from us, did he? I mean, in a way, that's a bit of a comfort. In some of these science fiction stories, they make it sound like human beings are going to be monsters, or robots, in the future.'

'There's one thing he did say: he said he lived in the Age of Simplification. He made it sound like there had been lots of different ages between then and now, and it had gone a bit wild, so they were trying to keep things more normal.'

'I don't understand exactly how you talked to each other.'

'There's lots of it I can't understand. It just happened.'

'I do know it's changed you, though.'

'How do you mean?'

'You're much more grown-up because of it. It's really made a difference.'

'I feel just like I did before. Except I want to *know* more, especially about the sea and pollution and things like that.'

Ellen persisted. 'What are you going to do now?'

'I promised Mum we would write to Aunt Dorothy and tell her how to get here for the wedding.'

Ellen groaned. 'I'd almost forgotten! What a fuss just over a silly old wedding. I'm going to go off and get married in a registry office – that's *if* I get married.'

'You won't get so many presents,' Tim said practically.

'Who cares? Most of the ones Viv is getting are awful, anyway.'

Preparations for the wedding had been going on for so long, it seemed the actual day would never come. There were always packets and parcels lying about on the chairs, and sewing everywhere.

Mr Dunwoodie arrived home from a business trip in time to order some more drinks, buy a new pair of shoes, get his hair cut, and try to prepare his speech. Tim very wisely stayed out of his father's way during this trying time, and nothing was said about the business of Edwin and the future poisoned sea.

Tim was bought a new suit that he secretly thought was marvellous. He went round to show it to Grandfather, and found him very busy too. He was making a small, inlaid workbox for the bride's wedding present, and it was a pleasure to watch as he lovingly polished each fine piece of rosewood and pear, and fitted them together.

'Not that I'll be there,' he declared. 'Can't stand crowds of relations, all saying nasty things about each other behind their backs.'

'But you've got to be there,' Tim insisted. 'You're the head of the family.'

Grandfather looked pleased about that. 'Well,

I'll see how my arthritis is. If it's playing up, I won't go.'

In fact, he did. And so did Uncles Harold, Arthur and Will, and Aunts Violet, Dorothy, Emma and Jane, with all their children and grandchildren too. And all the bridegroom's family was there, and all the friends of the two families. Almost half the village packed the church. Tim and his mother sat in the front row of the pews on one side of the church, and the bridegroom's mother and father sat on the other. Tim found there were all sorts of rules about weddings. The bridegroom had to stand and wait at the altar with someone called the best man, and then the organ played, and the bride came up the aisle on the arm of her father, followed by Tess, Pauline and Ellen in their bridesmaid's dresses. He hardly recognized any of them, especially Viv, the bride.

After the service, photographs were taken on the church steps, and Tim pulled a face in the ones that included him. Then they were taken by cars to the village hall, although it was only a few hundred yards away.

They ate chicken and ham salad and trifles and jellies, and drank white wine. Then he was given a glass of champagne with a tiny piece of the wedding cake.

'Don't drink it yet, you daft thing!' Ellen hissed. 'You have to wait for the toast.'

He looked around, but could not see any

toast. Then he was glad he hadn't said anything, because he found out that 'toast' meant a lot of boring speeches by the bridegroom, his father, and the best man. Then Grandfather got up to say a few words. And only then was he free to leave the table and talk to his cousins. They found quite a lot of glasses with drink still in, and Uncle Arthur gave him a glass of beer.

Mrs Dunwoodie stood near the door, smiling at everybody, really, it had been worth all the effort; a really wonderful wedding it had been. No one had been rude to Aunt Jane, who could be very touchy at times, and Uncle Will had not drunk too much.

Even Tim seemed to be having a good time. He had been looking too quiet lately, but perhaps the wedding would help get that other business out of his mind. No sense in troubling John with the story now, he had enough on his mind with the worry and expense of the wedding. The whole thing would blow over, she was sure, and Tim would settle down and be his old self again.

Back home, later that night, Ellen sadly took off her pale blue dress with rosebuds round the neck, and carefully hung it up at the back of her wardrobe. Tim stopped to watch her, on the way to his own room.

'Did you enjoy it, El?'

'It was lovely. Did you?'

'Mmm. The food was all right. But what a *performance*!'

Ellen laughed and said, 'Well, your friend Edwin would have enjoyed it. That's what he calls social history, isn't it?'

'I suppose. Do you think they will do things differently in four hundred years from now?'

''Course. They won't be tying old boots on the back of jet-packs or rockets, will they?'

'I didn't ask him about churches. That's something else they might not have. What do you think, El?'

But Ellen would not commit herself one way or the other, and soon each went to bed.

9

The Competition

It was just before the science lesson, and the teacher took Tim on one side.

'That was a nice bit of work you handed in, Tim.'

He could feel himself blushing. 'Really?'

'Are you keen on science?'

'I think so, I'm not sure really.'

'I expect it's all a bit new yet, but you show promise.'

Tim felt shy and yet pleased to be singled out for such praise.

'I've got something to tell you all,' said the teacher, Julie Noakes, raising her voice, 'so settle down. Let's have some quiet.'

When the class was giving her at least part of their attention, she held up a magazine for them to see.

'I don't know if any of you have ever seen this. It's a monthly magazine called *Scientific Knowledge*. Anyone read it?'

One or two of them put up their hands hesitatingly.

'Good. Then you'll know it tries to make science popular and easy to understand.' They groaned.

This month the magazine is setting a competition for boys and girls under sixteen, and I thought you might like to have a bash at it.'

'What sort of prizes are they giving?'

'First prize is a hundred pounds.'

They whistled and laughed. 'Tell us how to get rich!' . . . 'It's worth having a go, then.' . . . 'What's it all about?'

'Be quiet, and I'll tell you. The subject they have set is, "Living in a Computer Age".' There were more groans.

'All right. I know it's difficult. But if any of you want the details, come and see me after the lesson.'

Tim was one of the pupils who copied the details into their exercise books. He knew exactly what he was going to write. Instead of going home after school, he sat in the library and wrote for about half an hour without stopping. At Mrs Nelson's shop in the village, he bought a big envelope and a stamp. There and then, he posted off his entry to the competition: 'Living in a Computer Age – in AD 2500.' It caught the six o'clock post.

'I didn't even read it through,' he thought later. 'Oh, well. It won't win, anyway.'

Victor was free for some serious skate boarding, and Tim forgot to tell Ellen about the competition.

Because Normancote was near the sea, the Dunwoodies often took the opportunity, when the weather was fine, to go to the beach early in the day, before the day-trippers filled it up. One Sunday in late September, when a hazy but hot sun shone, it was decided to beat the traffic and head for the sea.

'If we all do something, we can leave in about half an hour,' Ellen said eagerly.

'Can Grandfather come too?' Tim asked.

'We don't want to go, do we, Tess?' Pauline said. 'We're going to be busy.' They both giggled, and Tim looked at them with contempt.

'Out with those boys again! All right, that means there will be plenty of room for Grandad, if he wants to come.'

Tim raced upstairs to make his bed and get his swimming things. He knew the sea would be cold, but it was worth going in, all the same. He put his cricket ball and bat in the duffle bag along with his towel and trunks and felt excited. It was going to be a lovely Sunday!

They collected Grandfather on the way, and because they reached the sea so early, the beach looked fresh and clean as the tide went out. There was a cold wind, but the sea sparkled and glistened whenever the sun came out. They kept warm after a quick dip in the big waves by running about, and playing French cricket.

At about midday, Grandfather got up stiffly from his deckchair and gave Tim a wink. 'Coming for a little stroll?' he asked.

Tim nodded eagerly. He knew exactly what that meant; it meant they would walk along the front to one of the old pubs, and sit down outside on a bench. Grandfather would have a pint of ale, and he would have a lemonade and some crisps.

They climbed over a breakwater, the old man very stiffly. 'Whoever invented deckchairs couldn't have ever sat in one,' he grumbled. 'I'm glad to stretch my legs.'

'Never mind, Grandad. Aren't you glad you came?' They looked at the sea, at the birds squealing overhead and at a line of small sailing boats getting ready to start a race.

'Takes a morning like this to make you realize what your friend Edwin's had to give up.'

'I'd almost forgotten,' Tim said, guilt flooding him because of it. 'I thought you had, too.'

'Well, so I had, but there was something in the paper this morning reminded me.'

'What?'

'Here. I've got it on me.' He pulled a much-folded newspaper out of his back pocket. 'You read it.' They sat down outside the *Rose and Crown*. 'I can't see without my glasses.'

'But you're wearing them!'

'Not these glasses. These are my wearing glasses. I mean my reading glasses.'

Tim shrugged and started to read the article Grandfather pointed to.

'Dr Paula Mackenzie, zoologist of Oxford University, claims that dolphins dance. In an article in the current issue of *Nature*, Dr Mackenzie reports on the habits of the Mediterranean dolphin, which she studied for five months last year off the Greek coast. She describes their behaviour and social habits, and suggests that, at certain times, their swimming movements fall into curious patterns.

"It is like some sort of ritual dance," she writes. "I have seen several individuals in a school repeat these movements over and over again. The action seems unrelated to courtship ceremonies, nor does it seem to constitute part of their 'games'. It is as if the animals were performing a dance-drama in front of their companions."

'Gosh,' said Tim. 'Like Edwin said it would be! I wonder if this Doctor is the person he meant, when he said someone found out about the dance four hundred years ago.'

Grandfather disappeared to get their drinks and two packets of crisps. Then they sat looking out at the green and silver sea.

'It's awful to think it's all going to change,' Tim said sadly.

'Don't worry. We'll beat it yet,' Grandfather said firmly.

'I've been reading a bit about dolphins, Gran-dad. They're so – interesting! Did you know dolphins have saved people from drowning by giving them rides on their backs?'

'No!'

'It's true, they really seem to like us. And scientists say their brains are as big as human brains, so they must be clever.'

'Well, all that time I thought they were no more clever than fish.'

'They talk to each other, too. They make different clicking sounds.'

'You *do* know a lot.'

'And people are trying to get the law changed, so dolphins don't get caught in the nets that tuna fishermen use in the Pacific.'

'How can they stop that?'

'By using different nets, I suppose. I'm not quite sure, but Mum says you can buy tins of tuna now that say they contain tuna that doesn't harm dolphins.'

'It seems to me people are beginning to get the message.'

'What message?'

'That you mustn't kill the goose that lays the golden egg.'

Tim didn't follow this, he just nodded.

'Are you going to help me again, then?'

'I'm all for a bit of a fight. You know me.'

'But what can we do?'

'We can go back to your mum and get some

food. That's what we can do. I'm starving, aren't you? Just leave the thinking to me.'

They did not speak about Edwin and the dolphins any more. It was just an ordinary autumn day by the sea. At the back of Tim's mind, helping him to appreciate the simple things they did, was the thought that one day all this would be poisoned. It made it all seem more special.

10

A Ship Goes Down

The next night, Tim sat biting his fingernails, trying to do his homework.

'El, what was the Thirty Years' War all about?'

Ellen pretended not to hear.

'ELLEN.'

'Oh, leave me alone, can't you? I've got my own work to do. And it's harder than yours. If you don't know, you'll just have to tell your teacher you can't do it.'

'Oh, yes, very funny,' he jeered. 'Just like you, I suppose, when you couldn't do your geometry and cried all over the place.'

'Mum, tell him to shut up!'

'Stop it, you two,' she said calmly, not taking her eyes off the television programme she was watching. 'Your father went to a lot of expense, buying that set of encyclopaedias. I can't think why he bothered – none of you ever look anything up in them.'

Tim went over to the bookshelves. 'What shall I look under? Thirty?'

Ellen raised her eyes to the ceiling. 'No. Try looking it up under twelve and three quarters.'

He pretended not to hear this. 'Thargelia . . . what on earth is that? Here we are – Thirty Years' War.' He read for a few moments, then started to flip the pages again. 'Hey, these books aren't bad. There's pages and pages about the theatre. Drawings and everything. And there's thermodynamics . . .' When their homework was finished, Tim took down a different volume of the encyclopaedia, chose the juiciest looking apple in the fruit bowl, and kissed his mother good-night.

'What's that you've got?'

'An apple.'

'No, silly! I mean the book.'

'It's a bit of the encyclopaedia.'

His mother looked pleased. 'Well, don't read too long.'

Up in his tiny room, he quickly got ready for bed, and then drew the heavy book on his knee. It must have weighed pounds.

'What a weight. Lucky old Edwin keeps all his books on his head!' he thought, opening the encyclopaedia at the page he wanted. There it was . . .

'*Dolphinus delphis* . . . black above, white below . . . about six feet long . . . makes noises, both as a language and supersonically . . . has between 160 and 200 teeth . . . follows ships . . .'

Not much there, really. Tim bit into his apple and thought about Beppo. Edwin had said they had not met any other form of life from outer space. It was funny to think how much time and energy people spent rushing off to planets and the moon, trying to discover things, when all the time, right here under the sea, waiting for the right questions to be asked, was a really intelligent creature.

Breakfast at the Dunwoodies was always a hurried affair during the week. John Dunwoodie was the only one who seemed to have time to have two cups of coffee and read the paper.

'A boat's sunk.' He read from his paper. '"Disaster at Sea. The 5000 ton merchant vessel, *Honour Bound* is feared to have sunk in mid-Atlantic in the early hours of this morning. She was still ablaze from stem to stern, in the first light of dawn."'

He looked up. 'Seems funny, a fire at sea. You'd think with all that water about, it wouldn't have a chance to catch hold.'

'Was it an old ship?' Tim asked, not terribly interested, but wanting to be polite.

His father went on reading. 'No, she wasn't. It says she only went into service fifteen months ago. Here, you'd better read it yourself. I'll be late.'

He threw Tim the paper, and grabbed hold of Ellen to give her a kiss, as she came flying into the kitchen, late for breakfast.

'When will you be back, Dad?'

'Friday. Be a good girl.' He shouted goodbye as he disappeared out the front door, struggling into his raincoat.

She started to sing along with a tune on the radio, but stopped when she saw Tim's face. 'Hey, what's the matter? You look terrible!'

He seemed not to hear. He picked up the paper, which had somehow got dropped in the milk, and disappeared upstairs to his room. There, he sat down on his bed, and read again the words that had made him turn so pale.

"The ship's owners say her cargo was a mixed one. Apart from several cases of Irish whiskey and some farm machinery, the *Honour Bound* was carrying the first consignment of car bodies made from a new wonder plastic: Tribaxin."

Tribaxin. And the *Honour Bound* had sunk in mid-Atlantic. And Edwin had said that the poisoning had started from the mid-Atlantic.

'It's just got to fit,' he said, seeing his sister standing at the door.

'What's got to fit? What are you talking about?'

'Oh, it's so difficult to explain. It's about this boat that sank last night. It had Tribaxin on board, and Edwin said the word Tribaxin to me. I'm sure it was a warning.'

'I don't understand a word you're talking about.'

'Look here. Read it for yourself. Then I'll try and explain.'

A few minutes later, Ellen and Tim sat together, looking very thoughtful.

'Let's have a look at the atlas. Have you got one?'

Ellen fetched her atlas from her satchel. They studied the map of the Atlantic Ocean.

'Look. If the boat sank anywhere about here, it could easily get stuck down in one of the valleys and not drift about too much. The poison would get carried this way by the currents.'

'But we don't know it was the Tribaxin. We don't even know the boat did sink in that part of the sea.'

Tim set his mouth in a thin line of determination, and when he spoke, it sounded like a vow. 'I don't know yet. But I'm going to find out. And I'm going to try and stop any more of this stuff getting thrown about.'

Ellen was impressed. 'Do you think we could start by ringing somebody up and finding out exactly where the boat did sink?'

They thought about it for a moment.

'Listen,' Ellen said at last. 'I'll do it. I'll ring up the owner – it gives their names here – and pretend I'm a reporter on the *Kent Messenger*. Then we'll get some more details to work on.'

'Would you? Could you?' Tim was a little scared. But Ellen was not. She had really entered into the spirit of the thing by the time she reached the telephone. She asked Directory Enquiries, in a very grown-up way, to give her the number of

76

the Roberts Line in Trafalgar Square. 'Here goes,' she whispered, as they heard the telephonist at the other end answer, 'Roberts Line. Good morning.'

'Oh, hello. I want to speak to your Press Officer, please. He isn't in? Is there anyone else there I can speak to, I'm from the *Kent Messenger*.'

There were a few clicks on the line, and Ellen gave her brother a triumphant wink. Then she spoke again into the mouthpiece.

'I'm enquiring about the *Honour Bound*. I want to know if any local men were hurt or lost at sea. No one was? Oh, that's good. It would help my story, though, if you could tell me exactly where she went down.'

She signalled wildly for a pen, and wrote some figures down on the telephone book cover.

'Thank you. Yes, I've got that. You've been most helpful. Goodbye.'

Tim slapped her on the shoulder with glee. 'It worked! What did they say, El? You sounded just like a reporter, you were great!'

Ellen leaned against the wall, looking quite shaky now the phone call was over.

'Here, I wrote down the latitude and longitude – now we'll see exactly where it went down.'

They rushed upstairs to look at the atlas again. Tim made a small pencil cross where the longitude and latitude met. They looked at each other.

The *Honour Bound* had sunk just above the deepest part of the mid-Atlantic Ridge, slightly to the west of the high and low currents that flowed towards Europe.

'That proves it. That's good enough for me,' Tim said. 'The poison started from there, the Tribaxin went down there. It must be what Edwin meant.'

'You'll have a hard time convincing people it's a poison.'

Somewhere a clock struck the half-hour. Ellen jumped. 'Is that the time? I'll be ever so late for school. Let's leave it until tonight.'

'Crikey! I'll be late as well!' Tim grabbed his satchel and flew downstairs. He had his cycle out of the shed before Ellen had reached the kitchen door.

'See you tonight, then,' he called, wobbling off down the road.

'Yes, 'bye,' Ellen called, struggling into her blazer and hoping her school bus would be as late as it usually was.

On the steep hill down to his school, Tim wheeled the bike into the gutter and stopped. He sat on the saddle, balancing with his toes, and gave himself up to deep thought. Then he came to a decision.

'No. I won't go to school. I can't just go on as if nothing had happened. Even if it does mean trouble, I've just got to get this thing sorted out.'

Before he could change his mind, he turned his front wheel round and pedalled as fast as he could back to the crossroads. There he took the left fork that led to Shenton and Grand Universal Laboratories.

11

Grand Universal Again

'If I don't do something, there's no one else will,'
Tim muttered to himself, as he chained his bike
to the car park railings. He kept saying it. It gave
him a little courage.

The receptionist was at her desk, but seemed
not to remember him.

'Is Mr Crossfield in?'

'Mr Crossfield is a very busy man.'

'Please, it's ever so urgent.'

She relented. 'All right. I'll see if he's free.'

She dialled a number on her telephone and
leaned across to Tim. 'What shall I say?'

'Say Tim Dunwoodie wants to see him.' She
talked into the telephone, then said, 'Well, it
seems all right. Take the lift. Third floor, room
305.'

He thanked her and got into the lift. He had
never worked one like this before, and he hoped
he had got it right. He pushed a button with

'3' on it, and the doors whooshed shut and he felt himself rise. He got out and almost ran down the corridor to room 305, not daring to give himself time to turn round and go back to school.

'Come in,' said Mr Crossfield.

He was sitting behind a very untidy desk. Through a door to the right, Tim caught a glimpse of a woman in a white coat, busily putting together something that looked like an animal cage with a television set inside it. It looked very interesting, but Tim did not have time for that now.

'Hallo, Tim.' If Mr Crossfield was surprised to see him, he managed to hide it, and his smile was friendly as he told Tim to sit down and make himself comfortable.

'Have you come on your own?' he added, as Tim still could not find anything to say.

'I didn't tell Grandfather I was coming. I had to see someone urgently, someone who could help, and I thought of you.'

'Nothing wrong, I hope? You sound upset.'

'I want to get some help. It's about Tribaxin.'

Mr Crossfield's eyebrows rose an inch. 'Tribaxin. The new plastic? Didn't you mention it before? I don't quite see . . .'

'Please, Mr Crossfield, I don't know who else to go to. I've told the story to Grandfather and my mother, and my sister. But they aren't experts or anything. I thought you might be able to help, because you're a scientist, and perhaps you can stop them making any more.'

Mr Crossfield opened his mouth, but said nothing. He could see that Tim was very distressed, but he had no idea what he was talking about.

After a moment, he said, 'Until you explain, I don't know if I can help or not. Suppose you start at the beginning?'

This is it, Tim thought. The moment he had dreaded, when he would have to tell a stranger all about the meeting with Edwin.

'Some time ago, a few weeks back, I went for a walk. Call it a dream, or whatever you like, but I met a boy and he said he was from the future, and he told me they could get in touch with each other telepathically in his time, because they wore sort of computers on their heads. I could see him as clear as I see you, and I could see these knobs on his head, the computers. He said his had suddenly got twisted up and gone wrong, and somehow he had come back into our time, four hundred years back.'

'How did you speak to each other?'

'Like normal and with telepathy. That's how I'm sure it was real and not a hoax. I mean, I really felt this telepathy.' Tim stopped in surprise. Mr Crossfield was sitting there, his eyebrows going up and down, but he believed him!

'Go on,' he urged.

'Well, he told me something that was terrible.

He said that the sea was poisoned in his time, and no one could work out what it was. It wasn't anything usual, and it worked by what he called a chain reaction, so it got worse and worse. He told me about how the fish were all dying, and the dolphins. He had a pet dolphin, you see, and it hurt him very much to see it dying.'

Mr Crossfield got up from his chair, and beckoned a white-coated woman into the room, but he was still listening intently.

'Well, anyway, on the day I came to see you with Grandfather, I was sure I heard Edwin's voice, sort of calling me and trying to warn me about something. And he said this word, "Tribaxin", over and over again. I'm sure I've never heard the word before, and you said it was brand new, but I didn't somehow think it could have anything much to do with the poisoned sea. I didn't think it was important.'

When he said the word 'Tribaxin', the white-coated woman had jumped and looked at Dr Crossfield nervously. She now spoke.

'It's important all right, but I don't see how it fits into your story.'

'I didn't either, until today. You see, Edwin, that's the name of this boy, told me the poisoning started in the middle of the Atlantic, and drifted east. Last night a boat sank at exactly the right spot, and it was loaded with Tribaxin.'

'You think Tribaxin is the poison? It's just not possible. Plastics can't just turn into poison. At least, they haven't ever done so.' She started to pace up and down the room, her hands deep in her pockets.

Mr Crossfield looked quite pale.

'Have you ever heard the word, "benign"? Well, plastic is benign, it isn't malignant, like poison. And this one is supposed to be more benign than most – it's biodegradable. Do you know what that means?'

'It wouldn't have turned into a poison overnight. It took years and years. It might have got mixed up with something else in the shipwreck or in the sea. It's got to be Tribaxin. The word came into my head, and I'm sure it was Edwin's voice, and then it sinks in just the right bit of the sea like that . . .'

Tim's voice trailed away. It suddenly seemed to him quite an impossible and silly thing. He got up. 'I'd better go.'

'You stay where you are. You're not going until I've had time to think about it for a bit.'

Martin Crossfield pulled at his lip. 'Dora, did you keep the trials on Tribaxin in your filing cabinet?'

'I've got them somewhere. She slipped into the next room, and after a while returned with a folder. 'There's something about it here. What it's made of, how it's made, tests made on it, what you can do with it. Give me a minute, and I'll try and work something out.'

Tim sat and watched her making notes all over a

piece of paper. She was about Vivienne's age, he thought. When she stopped writing, she squinted and gave him a friendly grin. 'The scientists in the future are working on it, you say? So in the time since you spoke to Edwin and now, they may have got it beat.'

'I suppose they could have.'

'So whatever we do now, they may not need your help after all.'

'You mean, we may as well not do anything,' Tim said humbly, 'just in case they can stop it themselves?'

'Put like that, it sounds a bit cowardly. But, yes.'

'But Edwin went to a lot of trouble, I'm sure he must have, to get that message to me. He must have had a reason. Why should he have bothered if he thought they could do it themselves?'

Mr Crossfield and the scientist he called Dora said nothing for a while but then Dora seemed to come to a decision. 'All right. Good. We shall assume he needs help, and the responsibility rests with us.'

She looked at her notes again. 'I don't know . . . it might just be possible, if the reaction was over a long . . . Let me see . . .'

She made signs all over the paper, but it seemed to get nowhere.

'Another thing, Tim. If we stop making it at Grand Universal, someone, somewhere else, is bound to discover it sooner or later. That's the way science works. Then what could we do?'

'But if you proved it was dangerous, couldn't the scientists make it differently?'

'I can't say.'

'Who do you have to tell, if you think it *is* the poison?'

'There's only one person who says yes or no to things like this. That's the Managing Director of Grand Universal.' She smiled grimly. 'And no one tells him he's made a mistake — not if she wants to keep her job, that is.'

'Oh.'

'Yes, he's the man to see. Sir Arthur Bernard MacLeish.'

Tim stood up. His voice was wobbling a little, but he asked, 'Where can I find him?'

Mr Crossfield stared. 'You mean you're going through with it?'

'I've got to. If I don't, no one else in the world will.'

'He's upstairs on the fifth floor. I mean, that's where he is, if he's here. But he won't see you.'

Tim was already opening the door. 'I've got to try.'

Dora and Mr Crossfield stared at each other for a long moment. Then with a sigh, he got up from his desk chair, put down the pencil he had been fiddling with, and joined Tim. 'Come on, then. Let's get it over. What about you, Dora?'

'Sure, you can't keep all the fun to yourself!'

*   *   *

The fifth floor had thick, grey carpets on the floor and oil paintings on the walls. Mr Crossfield spoke in a whisper before opening a polished door. 'You leave all the talking to me, do you hear?'

Tim nodded. Having this man and woman help him was so wonderful, he felt almost brave. Inside the office, a calm, stately woman with grey hair sat behind a desk, and looked up from some papers when she saw the three of them. 'Mr Crossfield? Dr Tulley?'

'Is Sir Arthur in?'

She looked at them steadily. 'I can see no appointment in the diary,' and she looked over her glasses reprovingly at Mr Crossfield.

'There isn't one. I mean, I didn't make one. But I've got to see him today.'

They heard someone in the next room opening a drawer.

'No one, *no one* sees Sir Arthur without an appointment.'

'This time,' Mr Crossfield said firmly, 'they do!'

He took Tim's arm in a steely grip and pushed open the door of the Managing Director's office. Dora Tulley smiled bravely and followed them into the room.

There was a small, very fat man sitting behind the huge desk. He looked so surprised to see them, he opened his mouth wide. Then he closed it abruptly and pulled himself together.

Tim tried to hide behind Mr Crossfield, but covertly examined the Managing Director of Grand Universal Laboratories. He was very pink and shiny, with gold rimmed spectacles and very little hair. Fat bulged over the collar of his grey suit. His eyes were the same light grey, and cold as stone. His voice, when he spoke finally, was strong and deep, the voice of someone used to giving orders.

'What do you mean by barging in here? And who's that?' He pointed with distaste at Tim.

Mr Crossfield cleared his throat. 'Excuse me, Sir Arthur. I had to see you, because something important has come up. I wanted you to hear it straight away.'

'What's the boy doing here?'

'He has something to do with this – this discovery. It's about Tribaxin.'

'Go on.'

'Apparently a boat sank today carrying the first load of Tribaxin to the States.'

'You burst in here like a maniac to tell me that! I've had people phoning me since four o'clock this morning!'

'Yes, Sir. It's not the actual sinking I wanted to warn you about, but what the sinking may mean. We have reason to believe the Tribaxin may slowly deteriorate into a poison – it could be very serious.'

'What are you talking about? You haven't even been working on Tribaxin, have you? Where's your proof? Why are you here, Dr Tulley?'

'We haven't any proof. Not yet, anyway. If you give me time, I think I've got an idea of what may happen. I want to get working on it right away.' She was very pale, but kept her chin in the air as she spoke.

'Do you now?'

'And in the meantime, if you don't mind, Sir, I think it might be wise to stop making any more.'

Sir Arthur was so taken aback, he spluttered when he answered. 'Do you take me for a fool?'

'No Sir. Of course not.'

'Well, do you think we haven't tested this stuff? Do you think we don't make sure our products are safe? How dare you tell me my business.' As he paused for breath, Dora and Tim instinctively took a few steps back. Mr Crossfield looked as if he would like to sink into the ground.

'Do you know our record of safety? Our things are better tested, more thoroughly investigated, than anyone's in the world. If some silly fool takes too much of a medicine, he may get a rash, that's all.'

'We're not talking about a rash, Sir,' Mr Crossfield said, 'I'm talking about a serious chain reaction that could spread all over the sea.'

'So you tell me. With no proof whatsoever. I think you've taken leave of your senses, Crossfield, and you, Tulley. I really do. I've just told you, all our products are thoroughly tested.'

'There could be a slip-up. Something no one

thought to test.' He was a stubborn man, Mr Crossfield, but Tim knew it was no use.

'You've both got a good record here, otherwise I'd think seriously about your positions. This is no way for scientists to behave. Now get back to your work, and let me get on with mine.'

They backed out. Tim tried to think of something to say, especially as it looked as if the two scientists had ruined their careers for his sake. And they had all failed.

Dr Crossfield came with him to the front door. Dora Tulley mumbled her goodbyes. 'We'll work something out, you bet.'

'It's not your fault. I'm so sorry.'

'Get on home now. Or should you be at school? I'll be in touch if I think of anything . . .' Mr Crossfield looked shaken, but smiled.

'Don't give up hope.'

Tim tried hard to smile back, but failed. Then he slowly cycled to the corner that would take him back to school. At the last moment, he veered off in the direction of Grandfather's house. He couldn't face either school or home just then.

12

Letters

The old man was cooking his lunch when Tim arrived. He did not look terribly pleased to see his grandson.

'No school today?'

'I played truant.'

'Well, don't expect much of a dinner. There's not much in these packets.'

He divided the fish he had been frying between two plates, and added some mashed potatoes. 'Want some peas?'

'No. I'm not very hungry.'

But Tim ate the fish all the same, while he told Grandfather all about what had happened that morning.

'Business!' the old man exploded. 'I don't know what happens to people, when they get into business. Just because he's got lots of money wrapped up in this Tribaxin, that man will never change his mind. He won't care if he poisons all the seas between here and China so long as he makes a profit.'

'So, you see, its hopeless.'

'Course it's not. Big things don't come easy. Stands to reason you've got to fight harder for big things. Those boys at the top think they know everything, but they don't. We'll start by writing a letter to all the papers, and the people on the telly, and our MP . . . we'll show old Sir Arthur what's his name!'

One paper printed their letter, and one weekly magazine; seventeen others did not. They had a post-card from their MP, acknowledging their kind letter which would receive his attention. Tim was almost in despair.

'Weeks are going by! Doesn't anyone care?!'

'It looks bad, I admit,' Grandfather said. 'But we haven't tried the scientists yet . . .'

Grandfather loved a crusade. He looked ten years younger than he had at the beginning of their letter campaign. 'I'll get a list together and you can make some copies again.'

Tim was tired of the letter. He and Ellen had written it so many times, it no longer had any meaning. They had tried to type it on their mother's old portable typewriter, but they were so bad at it, they gave up.

They were in Tim's bedroom early in the evening, trying to do as many as possible before they got too bored.

'Let's stop,' Ellen urged. 'It's worse than writing lines. We've done twenty-seven of the beastly things, anyway.'

'OK.' He stretched to get the ache out of his hunched back. 'Thanks for the help.'

'I've been thinking. Do you think it would be better if you went to see someone else – better than writing these letters, I mean? Someone like the Prime Minister.'

'Ellen! I couldn't! Not after Sir Arthur.'

The truth was, Tim no longer felt brave or clever enough to convince anybody. He sighed. 'Sometimes I wish I'd never met Edwin, I really do.'

Ellen said nothing, but he knew she understood, which was a comfort.

His mother woke him up the next morning by calling up the stairs. 'Tim, come on down. There's a letter for you. It looks important.'

'Hang on!' He was excited and hopeful, but then he remembered they had used his Grandfather's address on their campaign letters. He took the envelope in his hands and turned it over. It said *Scientific Knowledge* at the top of the letter, and pinned to it was a cheque for £100.

'Dear Tim', the letter began. 'We are pleased to tell you that your entry for the "Living in a Computer Age" competition has been awarded first prize. The judges were very impressed by your imaginative essay, and they have decided to print your work in the next issue of *Scientific*

Knowledge, a copy of which will be sent to you later this month. We have much pleasure in enclosing a cheque for one hundred pounds, and take this opportunity to congratulate you on winning.'

His mother took the letter. 'May I see?' She gasped when she read it. 'Girls! Look here. Tim's won a hundred pounds!'

They all crowded round to see.

'We didn't even know you'd gone in for it. What did your essay say?'

'I can hardly remember it now. It was about people living in the future.' He stared at the cheque, still not believing he had won.

'What will you spend it on?'

'Is that why you've been up in your room, writing such a lot?'

'You are a dark horse!'

Tim tried to escape. 'I'd better take the letter to school and show Miss Noakes.'

'She will be pleased.'

But his science teacher knew about it already, because the entry had given the name of Tim's school, and the magazine had sent a letter to her, too.

Tim's winning essay was the subject of the Head's talk after Assembly Prayers that morning, and it was thrilling, and a bit embarrassing, to have his news told to the whole school. Afterwards a group of his form came up to congratulate him and ask questions about it.

'When can we read it?'

'In the next issue, I think they said. I didn't make a copy.'

Everyone had advice on what to spend his hundred pounds on. After a lot of discussion, Tim decided he would buy a camera.

For days afterwards, other pupils he hardly knew smiled at him, and told him about the different cameras they owned. It was a lovely week.

On the day his free copy of *Scientific Knowledge* arrived, he took it to school, and the essay was pinned on the notice board. He took it down a bit later to show it to Grandfather.

'Ah, you've brought it, then.' Grandfather took something out of his pocket and put it in Tim's hand. It was a crumpled up five pound note.

'Before I forget. Take this to add to your winnings. It costs a lot to get film developed these days.'

Tim stammered his thanks. He was very moved – he knew Grandfather only had his old-age pension to live on, and it was the first time the old man had given him a present of money.

'Don't make a fuss about it. You're a good boy, and it's about time I gave you a present.'

'Shall I read the essay, or fetch you your glasses?'

'You read it to me. Just let me settle myself. Right.'

Tim cleared his throat, and began to read. '"Living in a Computer Age – in AD 2500" by Tim Dunwoodie.

'"When we think about computers today, we think of big machines that are very expensive. They are generally found in big businesses, or in banks, and universities. When people have difficult questions to answer, they go to the machines and they can solve even the most difficult problem in less than a second. There are lots of different types of computers, but they are always fast, and cost a lot of money.

'"But must computers be so large? Lots of other machines started off by being big, and have got smaller. This is true of things like radios and television sets, so why not computers? One day a computer might be small enough to carry about, so that everyone could have one, like they have a watch or a pen today.

'"Computers cannot reason like the human brain does. This means they can only answer with a yes or a no. But in the future, perhaps the computer could be joined on to the human brain, so that the two work together. I think in AD 2500 people might wear computers on their heads, so that they can think like they do now, but have the advantage of a computer's speed and memory to give them the best of both worlds.

'"My teacher has told me that different parts

of the brain do different things. One part is for seeing, one part for the emotions, and so on. Nobody is quite sure about it yet, but in 400 years from now, they will have mapped out every bit of the brain, so each part could have its own computer. If that happened, the way people think might change. Not just get better and faster, but actually change into something different from the way our minds work today.

'"It might be possible to develop different parts of the brain, so that people can do things they cannot do now – such as telepathy.

'"If we saw someone with computers on their head, we would probably think it very strange and ugly. But to people in the future, it would seem as natural as wearing glasses."'

He looked up. 'That's the end.'

Grandfather took the magazine, put on his glasses, and read the whole thing for himself.

'Well, look at that. Your name at the top and everything.'

Tim felt a little bit embarrassed. 'The only thing is, I feel a bit of a cheat. I mean, everybody thinks I made it all up, but really it was just telling about Edwin.'

'Never mind about that. It's your essay, not Edwin's. It's not cheating to use what you know to your own advantage.'

'Don't you think so?' Tim was reassured.

'I think it's a very fine bit of writing.'

'It isn't really. I just wrote it down, didn't correct it or anything.'

'Well, you take it home and show your father. He's not seen it yet, you say?'

'No, he was away when it arrived. Mum said to take home your dirty washing.'

'That's good of her. Don't forget your fiver.'

'You bet I won't. I'm going to have a look at cameras on Saturday.'

'It's a good thing to have.'

'And the first picture I take will be of – guess who?' He laughed and went off home.

Miss Noakes stopped him after biology the next day. 'I've been meaning to ask you. How did you get the idea for your essay?'

'Oh, it sort of came to me one day when I was out for a walk,' Tim replied truthfully.

Before the competition, Tim had sometimes found it hard to make friends at school. The essay had changed all that. Everyone was friendly, and all the teachers knew him by name. After all, it had been worth going in for, just for the reputation it had given him. He found he was even enjoying his lessons more.

The weather was warm and sunny, not at all like November. Everything seemed to be back to normal; there were no more replies to their letters about Tribaxin. It seemed that the whole scientific world trusted Grand Universal Laboratories too much to take him seriously. Certainly the idea that a new plastic could turn into a deadly poison seemed to most of them the most ridiculous flight of fancy.

But sometimes Tim remembered. He felt again the pain and sadness of Edwin. He tried to explain the feeling one day to Ellen. 'We were so close, El. It was like being inside his brain.'

'And you really did feel all of each other's emotions?'

'Just as if we were one person.'

She considered this, and then said slowly, 'I sometimes feel as if I know what other people are thinking. Just in flashes, you know. I can't prove it, but it's enough to make me know how you must feel.'

'Oh, Ellen, I get really choked up sometimes when I think about Beppo, and all those other dolphins. I mean, it's worse even than losing a dog.'

Their mother came into the room. 'Tim, you've got another letter from the magazine.'

'Fan mail,' Ellen grinned. 'Come on, open it.' Tim opened the envelope.

'It isn't a fan letter. At least, I don't think so. They say a letter arrived for me, addressed to the magazine, and they've sent it to me.'

'Well what does it say?'

'Hang on, give me a chance! It says: "I have read your winning essay with a great deal of interest. It shows a knowledge of the research I am at present involved in, quite outside the normal grasp of a schoolboy. It raises doubts in my mind about the secrecy I had assumed surrounded my work, a project which you will understand is unique, and, to my knowledge, not being duplicated anywhere else in the scientific world."'

He stopped reading, and exchanged a surprised look with his mother.

'What does it mean?'

'It means this man, whoever he is, thinks you're pinching his secrets. Go on. There's more.'

'"I think it is imperative we meet, and would appreciate it if you would let me know when you are free to visit me at my laboratory in the near future." Signed Professor A. Hellebore.'

'Whatever will you do?' Ellen asked, aghast. 'He sounds ever so important. And ever so cross.'

'There's only one thing I can do. Tell him it's just a coincidence.'

'That's right,' his mother said. 'He's got to be told face to face it's your own idea, and you haven't ever heard of him, or his silly old research. Otherwise he could get nasty.'

They looked at the address at the top of the page. 'Hellebore Laboratories, Ashdean, near Cambridge.'

'But that's miles and miles from here. Do you think I should write to him first? Or go there?'

'Well, you can't go on your own, that's for sure,' said his mother. 'You're daft enough to get lost between here and Shenton, let alone Cambridge. I'd better go along too.' But she looked dubious. 'I can't ask for any more time off work – I had a lot off because of the wedding . . .'

'I could take Grandad, that's if he would.'

His mother looked relieved. 'That might be best.'

So Ellen and Tim took the letter to their grandfather's. He read it slowly, and listened to what Tim had to say. 'Of course I'll come.'

'Would you really? That would be great!'

'It's too far to get there and back in a day, anyway. We'd better ask the professor to find us somewhere to stay the night.'

'When shall we go?'

'It will have to be a Saturday, because of your school. Anyway, where is it? Is it on the railway?'

'Let's go and ask at the station,' Ellen suggested practically.

They were told by the local station-master that Ashdean was on a branch line from Cambridge. They were lucky; it was still open but due to be closed at the end of the year. They would have to go to London, cross the City to Liverpool Street Station, and then catch another train to Cambridge. It would cost a lot of money, and when they were told how much, Tim whistled.

'There goes my camera. It will cost even more if we have to stay in a boarding house overnight.'

Ellen was very angry for his sake. 'I think that

Professor is mean to ask you to go so far. He knew you were only a schoolboy.'

'But he didn't know where I live,' Tim answered, reasonably. 'He wrote to the magazine, remember.'

'That makes it worse. You might have lived in the Outer Hebrides for all he cared. Anyway, I've got about four pounds in the post office you can have.'

'No. I won't take your money.'

'What about asking Dad?'

Tim shook his head. 'It wouldn't seem right when I've got that money already.'

His mother was cross about it, too. 'All that fuss and expense! Why couldn't he have offered to come here?'

'Never mind. I'll write off and tell him to expect me and Grandad next Saturday.'

If Grandfather hadn't said he would go too, I'd not let you go after all.' His mother eyed him up and down. 'And you need new trousers – you've grown so tall in these last few weeks.'

'Hellebore?' Mr Dunwoodie said, very impressed when he read the letter. 'She's one of the most famous scientists we've got.'

'She?'

'Yes, I forget the first name, but I've seen her on a science programme on television.'

'I'll write the letter, if you like,' Tim's father said. 'What time did you say the train was?'

The Professor replied by return of post.

'Saturday would suit me very well,' she wrote. 'Any time of day will do, and you and your grandfather will be very welcome to stay overnight with me.'

That was one problem solved. And the Professor had solved another: inside her letter was a cheque that would more than cover the fare to Ashdean for both Tim and his grandfather. He wouldn't need to break into his hundred pounds after all.

'She sounds quite a nice woman,' he ventured to say to Ellen.

But privately he wondered about it. He had the sick feeling in his stomach all over again, like the day he had gone to Grand Universal. Still, he thought, she couldn't be much worse than Sir Arthur Bernard MacLeish.

13

Professor Hellebore

The hot journey to Ashdean Station finally ended at about half past three. It had taken a good part of the day to get there, because the trains ran to Ashdean only at three-hourly intervals, and they had a long wait at Cambridge for the branch line train. Tim was carrying a duffle bag with his pyjamas, toothbrush, and a clean sweater inside. He felt terribly hungry and thirsty, most of all thirsty. They had stopped at the station buffet for some ham rolls and tea, but that was all he had had since an early breakfast.

Grandfather wiped his forehead. He looked very cross. 'I hope this Professor of yours has got some tea on the go. Where's her letter?'

He took the paper out of his pocket and showed the address to the ticket collector.

'How far is it?' Grandfather asked, and the man pointed up the hill outside the station.

'Can't miss it, Guv'nor. Up on the right, a

few huts set back from the road. The name's on the gate.'

It was good to stretch their legs and breath the cold air after the long stuffy train journey. They found the gate, just as the ticket collector had said, with its hand-painted notice: 'HELLEBORE LABORATORIES. PRIVATE.'

Tim looked at the three, shabby huts. What kind of a person could Professor Hellebore be? His father had said she was famous, but this did not look like a famous scientist's laboratory. It looked like a collection of old cattle sheds.

Grandfather knocked on the peeling door and gave Tim a wink of encouragement. Inside, they could hear a radio playing pop music, and somehow this made everything seem more normal. Then the door opened.

The Professor held out her hand, first to Grandfather and then to Tim. 'So you've arrived. I'm so glad.'

She was a very short, very wide woman. She was wearing a dirty white coat, and running shoes. There was a streak of grease on one of her cheeks and she was holding a small spanner in her left hand.

'I expect you're ready for tea. I've got the kettle on.' Grandfather looked relieved and flopped on to a high stool just inside the door.

'I don't often have visitors here. I only come here for my private work. Most people come to see me at the University,' Professor Hellebore explained, as she busied herself putting out some doughnuts and buns on a plate and made the tea. 'If there were no buns,' she suddenly said, looking at the ceiling, 'it would be necessary to invent them.' Tim wondered why Grandfather laughed – he did not see why it was funny.

He looked about him. Grand Universal had given him a glimpse of what a large science laboratory looked like, but it had been nothing like this. Everything was in an indescribable jumble; there were wires trailing everywhere, and he had to duck under some to find a seat. There were saucers full of screws and nails, and pots of glue and paint, and piles of magazines on the floor (he caught a glimpse of the *Scientific Knowledge* that contained his article). There were computers and printers, and machinery Tim could not put a name to. On one wall, a blackboard used for chemical symbols had scrawled in the corner: 'Dunwoodies Saturday – get more milk'.

What a super place, Tim thought, and forgetting to be polite, helped himself to another bun and wandered about, poking into all the mysterious jumble.

The Professor and Grandfather seemed to be getting on together very well, and ignored Tim. He listened to the Professor answering a question about her work.

'This is my private work. Nothing to do with the University – I work here on my own. Some of the problems I'm tackling are very sticky . . .'

she licked some sugar crumbs off her fingers as if to prove the point.

'When I read Tim's article, I really had quite a jolt. I had to see him to find out how he had hit on the same idea as myself — it seemed too incredible that he hadn't heard it from somebody, and if he had, I wanted to know. A security leak at this stage might mean months of work for nothing, do you see?'

Her eyes were very keen as she looked at Tim. 'No one else in the world, as far as I know, is doing the same sort of work. So how you knew about it is a mystery.'

'Go on, Tim. You'd better tell the Professor about it.'

'I didn't make it up, but you might think so when I tell what happened.'

So once again Tim launched into the story of Edwin, and the strange computers he wore on his head. When he started to describe how they worked, the Professor stopped him.

'Tell me, what did they look like exactly? What colour were they?'

By her tone, Tim guessed this was a crucial question. He thought very hard, and in his mind's eye he could see how Edwin had looked, his bald head shining in the afternoon sun, and the headpieces wired into his head.

'They were sort of bluish, I think. Sort of like blue glass. I could see through them and sometimes they seemed to light up.'

107

The Professor looked at the blackboard. 'Can you draw them for me?'

'I'll try.'

He took some chalk and drew a semicircle, with one side flat and the other slightly jagged. Then he added a line, and said, 'The wire sort of disappeared into his head. They looked like that.'

The Professor stared as if at some masterpiece. 'So that's how it is. Of course, they would be . . .' Her voice trailed off, as lost in thought, she contemplated the chalked drawing. Then she clapped Tim fondly on the shoulder. 'Young man, I think you've saved me about six months' work. Like glass you say? Hmmm.'

She began walking round the laboratory in an excited fashion, and seemed quite to forget Tim and his grandfather. Then she took up some wires and bits of metal. 'To work, then,' she said softly.

'But I haven't finished telling you the story yet,' Tim cut in hurriedly. 'The bit in the story that worries us so.'

All the time Tim was telling her the story of the poisoned sea, the Professor kept busy with the wires. She seemed to be only half listening.

'So, after seeing the Managing Director, and writing all the letters, we didn't know what else to do,' Tim finished.

There was quite a long silence, and he glanced at Grandfather for support. The old man was just finishing his fourth cup of tea, and slowly filling his pipe.

'What do you think, then, Professor?' he asked.

'Don't smoke in here, Mr Dunwoodie, if you please. Think? I think it is entirely likely that this Tribaxin is the cause. Who can tell about these things? It might just as well be that as anything else.'

'I didn't mean that. I mean, what should we do now?'

'Nothing more you can do, I should think. Just hope they manage to sort it out for themselves in the future.' There was another silence. Tim felt himself grow red with disappointment. He was not sure what he had expected; in fact, he did not know he had expected anything until he saw how uninterested she seemed by the story. Then he realized he must have had an idea at the back of his mind that such an important scientist would somehow, miraculously, put everything right.

Grandfather got up and quietly stood by the Professor, as she still worked at the bench. He looked a little bit pink, too.

'It seems to me, Professor, that this is your fight now, as well as ours.'

She seemed surprised. 'How do you mean?'

'You seem to be very excited over what Tim has told you. Having Edwin appear like that, and having him wearing these things on his head and all, has showed how you aren't barking up the wrong tree. You said so yourself, knowing what they look like might save you months of work.'

'That's true.'

'Well, my point is, you owe him, this Edwin, something in return.'

Ann Hellebore put down the wires, and thought about what Grandfather had said. She sighed regretfully, but nodded in agreement. 'First things first, eh?'

'There'll be plenty of time for your computers,' Grandfather said equably. 'But just now, it would be very nice to have your help on the poisoning.'

'But I know nothing about plastics. Or the sea, for that matter.'

'Someone you know, perhaps?'

She thought for a while, then said, 'Pandie would be a good man, but he's in America. Cudlipp – no, he died last June. Bremlin and Todd are up the Amazon. Can't think of anybody else.'

She fixed her eyes again on the workbench. 'I suppose a name will spring to mind.'

Tim could not stop himself. Suddenly he burst out, 'We don't know anything about plastics, either! But we're trying to do something to help Edwin and the dolphins and everybody! You must know someone.'

The Professor looked at Tim with a new respect. The boy's concern had cut through to her at last.

'Perhaps the Minister can suggest someone – I'm dining with him this evening, in fact.'

'The Minister?' Grandfather asked breathlessly. 'What Minister?'

'The Minister of Science and Technology.' The Professor suddenly chuckled. 'Every now and then I go to see him, and he promises me another three feet of wire. We both get rude – but we're old friends, really.'

Tim could hardly stand such coolness. 'But don't you see? He's the very person to help!'

'Do you think so? Perhaps you're right. Someone with power *might* be more help than someone with knowledge at this juncture. And if you want power, don't come to me, or any other scientist, or the University for that matter. It's the Government that cracks the whip.'

'Hear hear,' said Grandfather, as if he were at a political meeting. Tim had not followed this little speech, but he saw the Professor was now willing to do something to help, and that was enough. He was suddenly flooded with new hope.

'Perhaps we'd better go now. The traffic can be very bad at this time of the evening.'

It took Tim a moment to realize that Professor Hellebore assumed that they were to go with her to the Minister's house.

'Won't he mind?' he asked.

'He might.' The Professor's face lit up with amusement. She looked a nicer, warmer person all of a sudden. 'But it would do him good to

111

meet someone like you for a change – someone with guts.'

'Come on, then,' Grandfather cut in. 'Don't forget our duffle bag.' And he added under his breath, 'And mind your manners when we get there!'

Meanwhile the Professor was changing out of her running shoes into a pair of brown brogues. She ran a comb roughly through her wiry hair. She removed the white coat and hung it behind the door. 'I'm ready when you are.'

A little bewildered, the two of them followed the Professor out of the laboratory, and wondered where they were to go: they had no idea where the Minister lived.

'I hope we don't have to go on another train. I've had quite enough for one day,' Grandfather whispered.

The Professor, however, led them to one of the other rusty huts, which turned out to be a garage. After the splendid cars Tim had seen outside Grand Universal, he felt a certain excitement. Professor Hellebore would have a very special car, he was sure – perhaps even a Rolls.

From inside the garage came a great bang and mechanical cough, and then the Professor slowly drove her car out for them to see. Grandfather put on his glasses to have a better look. He sighed nostalgically.

'What a beauty! A split windscreen Morris!'

'Had it practically all my life,' the Professor

smiled, as they climbed in. 'Still got the original leather seats.'

'Had one myself, when I was young', Grandfather said. Then they were off, and Tim listened to their talk about carburettors, petrol consumption, and the Morris Minor Club, for what seemed like miles and miles.

Half an hour later, although it seemed like more, he wondered if they would ever get to wherever they were going. The old car was croaking its way up every little hill, as if on its last gasp. It was very bumpy in the back and he felt slightly sick. Grandfather had gone quiet, so perhaps he felt queasy too.

At last the Professor signalled to turn left and slowed down. 'We're there,' she said.

14

At the Minister's

They came to a stop in the drive of a beautiful house. Thankfully, Grandfather heaved himself out of the car. 'That will teach me to feel nostalgic,' he said to Tim.

'At least we arrived. I began to think we wouldn't.'

It was fully night-time now. A small moon appeared and disappeared as clouds chased across the sky. An owl hooted away to their left in some trees, and there was a hint of frost in the air. From the house, bright warm light streamed from nearly all the windows, and it looked cosy and welcoming.

The front door was at the top of a small flight of steps, and it was opened almost at once by a woman who they later learned was the housekeeper.

If she felt any surprise at the sight of Professor Hellebore's companions, she managed not to show it. She bade them good evening and ushered the trio into the Minister's study. She told the cook a little later that there were two more scruffy-looking scientists for dinner.

'He's expecting you, Professor,' she had said, allowing herself very slightly to emphasize the 'you'. Ann Hellebore had already flung open the door, however, and announced her own arrival.

'Here I am, George,' she called pleasantly, 'come to cadge a few more bits of wire.'

It did not occur to Tim that this was a long-standing joke between them; he felt himself blushing at what he thought was the Professor's rudeness.

But the Minister laughed. All he said was, 'We'll see about that, Ann.'

The Minister of Science and Technology was a tall rather distinguished looking man in early middle age. Tim knew his face, he realized, from television interviews and photographs in the newspapers. In real life he looked smaller and more kind.

'Here are two new friends of mine,' said the Professor. 'Hope you don't mind me bringing them along. Mr and Master Dunwoodie.'

Tim felt grubby and untidy. He had never been in such a grand house. The furniture was beautiful, and the gleaming silver and gilded picture frames reflected in the light of a large, log fire. The Professor did not look exactly smart, either, in her roll-necked pullover and a tweed shirt. It would have been nice, too, if Grandfather had worn a tie with no egg stains on it.

It was a relief when the Minister said, 'I'm sure you all feel a bit dusty after your journey. I've been in that car, too!'. He laughed at the Professor, and showed them to a bedroom with a bathroom attached, where they got busy with large, expensive bars of soap, clean towels and clothes brushes. Tim brushed his hair for the first time that day, and it was an altogether neater looking trio that emerged. The Minister poured drinks for them all while he talked.

'What can I give you, Master Dunwoodie? Oh, good – your name is Tim, is it? Orange juice with soda is rather nice. And for you, Mr Dunwoodie? Ale? Certainly, I'm sure we've got some.'

The Professor had some sherry, and the Minister took a small glass of Madeira.

'Cheerio,' said Grandfather, and drank his ale down with a sigh of content. There was a small silence.

The Professor turned to the Minister. 'What did the Committee have to say?'

'I don't think you have to worry. They seem to think the work worth a grant. One or two doubted if you would get results very soon.'

'They'll get results all right – perhaps sooner than they think,' she said, and smiled at Tim.

The Minister saw the smile, but said nothing. There came the sound of a gong, which meant dinner was served, so they all went into the dining room.

The table was lit with two silver candelabra, and the knives and forks were heavy silver too. Grandfather winked at Tim, as if to say, 'Look at this, isn't it posh?'

The meal was just as grand as they had been led to expect. There were bowls of creamy soup, then venison steaks. Tim had never eaten venison before and thought it was quite delicious. He was given two glasses of wine with a little water added. The Minister looked at him and Grandfather a little curiously at times, but talked to Ann Hellebore about scientific friends, new discoveries and inventions, the disastrous by-election. Obviously, if the Professor did not want to explain why she had brought two guests with her, the Minister was much too polite to ask.

After a large helping of strawberry tart, Tim and the others went back to the study. Grandfather sat down in a corner near the fire. He could not keep his eyes open any longer. Tired from all the travelling and excitement of the day, unaccustomed to wine and large meals at such a late hour, the old man slumped further and further down in his chair, until a faint snore betrayed he had fallen asleep.

'He doesn't often have such a hard day,' Tim said to the Minister, defensively. 'We've been travelling since early this morning.'

The Minister just smiled, and looked at Grandfather. His hand caressed the head of an old Labrador stretched out at his feet, also asleep.

'You've come a long way, then?'

The question was put in such a way that Tim saw it was time for an explanation. He looked at his grandfather, then at the Professor, who simply gave a brief nod. One thing Tim was learning about Professor Hellebore – she always expected people to stand on their own feet, and she treated Tim, not as young boy in need of help and protection, but as another adult.

Tim did not feel at all like an adult just then. The large meal, the long day, the wine, all helped to make everything seem unreal. He could not concentrate on what he had to say. Yet he knew this was the chance he had been waiting for, his great opportunity to help Edwin and Beppo. He searched in his mind for words that might sway the Minister into helping him, words that would make him see what a terrible burden Tim had had to carry.

'Edwin!' he thought despairingly. 'If only you were here. You would know what to say!' But Edwin was not there. He had to do what he could, on his own.

'Yes, we have come a long way,' he finally answered. 'Professor Hellebore wrote to me and asked me to come and see her, because she thought I knew too much about her work. But that isn't why we came here, it's just part of it. You see, I've got to stop us from poisoning the sea.'

He stopped. The Minister, head on one side in

118

polite encouragement, looked at Ann Hellebore to see her reaction to all this.

Almost shaking with effort, Tim plunged on. 'About a month ago, I saw a boy. He said he was from the future. He *was* from the future, and he wore things on his head like the Professor is trying to make.'

'More or less the same,' was all the Professor said.

'Go on,' prompted the Minister.

'He told me the sea was poisoned and his dolphin was going to die.'

'His dolphin?'

'The Government's budget for the environment is pretty useless, don't you think?' the Professor said to no one in particular.

'This boy told me, later on, that they thought the thing poisoning the sea was something called Tribaxin. And then I found out Tribaxin was a new plastic. And a boat sank in the Atlantic with Tribaxin inside. So now I'm sure that's what done it.'

He blushed. The Minister would think him an ignorant little boy now, who could not even speak English properly. 'Did it, I mean.'

The Minister was still showing the same polite attention, whatever his thoughts might have been.

'Tribaxin? Yes, I've heard of it. Surely the makers have tested it? It's being made by a very reputable firm. Have you – have your family – contacted them?'

'I have. They said it couldn't possibly be Tribaxin. They said it is tested for everything.'

'What an extraordinary story.' The Minister spoke very kindly, but there was a note of finality in his voice as if to hint that he was a busy man and must not waste time on fairy stories. 'If the manufacturers are sure it isn't Tribaxin, then the poison the boy told you about must come from something else.' He shifted in his seat, as if he was getting a bit bored. 'Perhaps you should reconsider the whole thing.'

'It isn't something I just made up!' Tim felt tears of exhaustion and self pity pricking his eyes. But he was determined not to cry. HE HAD TO CONVINCE HIM! But how? He sent a silent and passionate cry from his heart out to Edwin. It was almost a prayer for help. There was certainly no help here in the room: Grandfather slept on, the Professor said nothing.

'Why don't they understand? It really is something important, it has to be, or why would they send a message over hundreds of years?' He turned to the Professor, but although she was listening intently, she did not intervene.

Tim looked at their kind but distant faces. Waves of loneliness swept over him. The lump in his throat stopped him saying anything more at all.

15

The Return of Edwin

Tim felt awful. This is how a footballer must feel, he thought bitterly, who misses a penalty in the World Cup. The Minister sat beside him, totally unconvinced by the story he had heard. And Tim couldn't blame him for that – he had not even told it well. After all, if an unknown, not very well-educated boy suddenly appears at your house for dinner, claims to have seen into the future, and without any proof at all expects the Minister of *Science* to believe him, well, he is asking for trouble.

These were Tim's bitter thoughts as they sat in the Minister's study. Each of them was silent for a long moment. The dog whimpered and shivered in his sleep; Grandfather twitched uneasily; a log fell with a shower of sparks further into the fire.

'It seems very cold all of a sudden,' the Minister exclaimed, getting up to put more logs on the fire. As he reached towards the fire-tongs, a chilly wind seemed to touch them all, blowing from every direction and yet from nowhere. The corners of the room seemed to fade away, until the four of them and the dog were enclosed in a ball of light that throbbed and shimmered all around them. It was as if they were trapped in a huge pearl, and a sensation of cold and shimmering light seemed to pass through them all for a second – three seconds, perhaps an hour: they had lost all sense of time. Even the Professor, trained to observe facts scientifically, had to confess afterwards that the clock seemed to blur and fade before her eyes, and even her own heartbeats were still.

They gaped at each other, not able to move or speak. Then, gradually, a warm, natural light returned. The slight noises of the room – the clock and the fire – could be heard again. It was no longer cold.

The Minister dropped the fire-tongs he had been holding and everything seemed to return to normal, to be the same as it had been a few moments (hours?) before.

Except for one thing. Edwin was sitting on the sofa.

He grinned, a conspiratorial and encouraging grin, at Tim. Then he stood up and bowed politely, first to the Minister and then to Professor Hellebore. His bald head and the headpieces flashed and gleamed in the firelight.

'Greetings. Please forgive me for intruding, but the Elders thought it might be necessary. They have sent me here to help my friend.' He glanced at Tim whose heart was leaping about in his chest with sheer joy.

'Oh, Edwin, I'm so glad to see you!' he exclaimed. The Minister closed his mouth, which had been gaping foolishly, and managed to stammer a welcome. Ann Hellebore took hardly any notice of anything that was said. Eyes popping, she stared at Edwin's microcybs.

'When I last saw Tim,' Edwin was saying, 'my arrival was purely accidental. A combination of faults in two of the microcybs projected me to your present, and my past, and so we met.'

'So he has said,' stuttered the Minister.

'Of course, coming back again to the correct time was very difficult. What was once done by mistake had to be repeated deliberately.'

The Professor nodded vigorously. 'Scientific progress is often like that. A mistake, an accident, opens up a new field. Then you have to find out what you actually did to make the discovery.'

Edwin laughed. He was standing now in front of the fire, graceful and at ease. There was nothing of the young, inadequate boy about *him*. He spoke to them all as equals.

'I want to tell you, Professor Hellebore, that your time is known to us as the Age of Amateurs. We know that many of the discoveries you made were random and unplanned, just as we know they led to many unplanned and evil side effects.

123

They were mere stabs in the dark. We, in our time, are not used to dealing in errors.'

The Professor looked furious, then sulky. She did not like to be called an amateur. After a moment's reflection, however, she saw that Edwin had not meant to be rude. He had simply said the truth as he saw it.

'I won't quarrel with you, young man. But you must have repeated your error, all the same, otherwise you wouldn't have appeared just now.'

Edwin shook his head. 'No. We found it impossible to transfer again.'

The others looked at him in surprise.

'How did you get here, then?' Tim asked. 'If you couldn't do it, how did you manage it?'

Edwin grinned at him again. 'First of all, you must understand that I am not here. Not really. The real me is still in my own time. I am some sort of mirror image of myself, rather like a beam of light, or a thought, but I don't expect you to understand.'

'Telepathy is the nearest word we have,' the Minister said.

Edwin nodded. 'That too. Let me explain how I came. I did not come by the power of my own brain – and certainly it was no error this time.'

He sat comfortably next to Tim, and began to tell them some of the difficult times he had had since his last meeting with Tim. In some ways it was a repetition of his friend's: he had found it difficult to convince people it had really happened, and that a contact with the past had been made. Of course, he found it was made easier for him by using his telecyb, and opening his mind up to those around him. Some of the experiences he had had with Tim could be 'read' telepathically. He had tried to convince his parents and his teachers how important it would be if he could only go back again to try and stop the manufacture of Tribaxin. His family had seen it as a waste of his brain's energies, just at the time he needed to concentrate most on his Big Examinations. And his teachers pointed out that, as the poisoning had already happened, and was in their seas, it was too late to do anything by going back again. The fish were dead, the dolphins dying. The poison existed. But Edwin was obstinate. By huge efforts of will, entirely on his own, he had somehow contacted Tim with just those few words: 'Tribaxin, Tim, Tribaxin'. But he could not manage any more.

He went on, 'My own power was limited, but I could not believe there was nothing else I could do. You see, my pet dolphin, Beppo, was dying.'

They were all engulfed with the boy's tender love and grief for his dolphin. The Minister instinctively reached out and caressed the head of his dog, who thumped his tail twice, although he was still asleep.

Grandfather slept on as well. It was very strange, he told Tim afterwards, but he remembered every second of the visit from Edwin, just as if it had been a most vivid dream. Sleep, apparently, was no barrier to this particular form of telepathy.

'Whatever did you do?' the Professor asked, hoarsely. She was obviously moved by the strength of Edwin's pain – just as Tim had been before her.

'I managed to gain an interview with one of the Elders. He listened to me most kindly. He also told me I could not alter the course of history. The poison, he said, existed. I could not make it cease to exist.'

Edwin seemed to blur and waver before them, as if he was tiring. Then he became clear and distinct again. He continued, 'I must not talk too much about the Elders. This will be understood by you when I explain how I am "with" you.

'The Elder I spoke to took me to four others. Between them they came to a decision which gave me a final chance. The Elders do not wear microcybs, but can do many things without them. They are different, and understand things more than we do. Together they are giving me the power to come back to you. In fact, the five Elders are standing round me now as I talk, and they say it could not be done without my own special strength. They say it has to be me that speaks to you, because of my attachment to Beppo. Do you see? I care so much about him, I'd do anything to save him.'

They did see.

'So the Elders don't want me to speak about

them, for that would bring their thoughts into the room as well as my own. They say this could not help solve the problem. They are quite firm about it.' He spoke as if he were listening to another voice giving him directions.

'So you are here because of the Elders, and not because of the microcybs?' said Tim.

'Precisely.'

'How did you find me?' Tim asked, puzzled. 'I'm nowhere near the Dell. Even I don't know where I am, exactly.'

'Where you were did not matter, once your individual personality had been "read" by the Elders from my telepathic picture of you. Everyone is unique. That means there never has been, nor ever will be, anyone quite like you. They found you, because you are the only Tim Dunwoodie.'

Edwin waited, as if he expected more questions. Indeed, all of them were dying to find out as much as possible before the inevitable time came for Edwin to fade away. The Minister spoke next.

'Forgive me for asking a question which may offend the Elders. I think it may only bring them in indirectly. What I should like to know is, what kind of government do you have in your day? Are decisions and laws made by the Elders?'

Edwin shook his head. 'Oh, no. The Elders are not representatives of anybody. They are just themselves. They serve just by thinking, and anyone can ask their advice. Our government is sort of like yours. But since the use of telepathy, the way we choose our representatives has had to change.'

'Why is that?'

'In your time, Minister, there are two main parties and several others, and one party has the power for a while and makes the laws while the others try to stop them, or change them. Right?'

'That's right,' he agreed.

Edwin looked as if he was enjoying himself. 'Often your representatives make promises to get elected, and say many fine things. To gain power, they are prepared to tell lies. Is this true?'

'Well . . .' The Minister did not know what to say.

Edwin laughed. 'Oh, I'm sure *you* don't lie, Minister, and I'm sure there are more honest people than dishonest ones, even in your Parliament.'

The Minister looked uneasy, just as the Professor had, some little time earlier, when she had been called an amateur. But in the end, he too agreed that Edwin was right.

'When telecybs were invented, do you see, people could not gain office by saying one thing and thinking another. This was true about the Government, and business and just about everything. They had to use new criteria for electing leaders or representatives. The things that matter now are things like wisdom, concern for others, honesty and intelligence. Speech-making no longer counts. So I think you can see,' Edwin finished, a little slyly, 'our choices are a little different from yours.'

The Minister shook his head as if to clear it, and then joined in the laugh that Ann Hellebore had started.

'Absolutely fascinating! No more cunning old foxes in Parliament. What a prospect! But where do they all go?'

They all laughed again. 'There aren't so many of them now. If you can't lie to gain your own ends, then you soon learn to become honest.'

The Professor leaned forward to gain Edwin's attention. 'Please, may I ask you a question? About the microcybs?'

'I think so.'

'Why do they glow and wink in that way?'

'It's the energy produced in the heliostites.'

'Heliostites?'

'Oh, of course, you haven't discovered them yet.'

Edwin shook his head regretfully, and although the Professor pleaded with him to tell her how to make them, Edwin stayed firm.

'I cannot say anything that is going to help you too much in the future. Surely you can see that that would be tampering with history. And I musn't do that.'

'But you've been telling the Minister all about your Government.' The Professor almost wailed with disappointment.

'No, really, I haven't said anything that would change history. All I have said about telepathy would have occurred to all of you, given time and common sense. It would be quite different to reveal scientific formulae.'

And nothing the Professor said would make him budge an inch.

Tim now found a chance to put in his questions. He knew there were a million things he would wish he had asked when it was too late, but while they were together, all he really wanted to know about were things to do with Edwin himself.

'How's Beppo? Is he all right?'

Edwin was able to smile, although a little sadly, and answered that Beppo was only a little worse than he had been before.

'I've learned such a lot about dolphins since I met you. And Ellen – that's my sister – has taught me a lot about all the pollution and things we're doing wrong.'

Again Tim felt the strong emotional joining that he had felt when Edwin first told him about his dying dolphin. That feeling was the basis of all that had happened. Without it, he wouldn't have had the strength to go on. And if Beppo died, if Beppo couldn't be saved, would it all have been worth it? As Tim thought this, Edwin smiled at him.

'I know you care, Tim. Believe me, you have been – magnificent!'

Tim felt himself blush. He quickly changed the subject.

'You know when we met that first time? And you were going to a history exam? Does that mean you want to be a history teacher when you grow up?'

Edwin's image blurred a little, but he answered clearly enough. 'I want to be an Elder. I know, of course, you can't try to be one. Either one's brain develops along certain lines or it doesn't. You can't make it happen.'

Edwin thought a little more. 'When we met before, I told you how I feel about the sea and the dolphins. Of course, I remember what the sea used to be like, before the poison. It's only possible now in the Pacific and parts of the Indian Ocean to go on with scientific research, and sea-bed farming. Still, I would like one day to do something like that – to be an oceanographer.'

They had all asked Edwin questions. They sat in silence, remembering why they were all together. His talk of the sea had reminded them.

'So all the seas aren't poisoned yet?'

'Not yet. The Pacific is almost completely free of it, and only parts of the China Seas and Indian Ocean are affected. Which is just as well,' Edwin added wryly, 'because most of the food eaten in Asia comes from the sea. When – if – the poison reaches that far, millions of people may starve.'

The Minister spoke quietly. 'You are sure it is this Tribaxin?'

'We are. When it started filtering out from somewhere in the Atlantic, there was a change

131

in the chemical structure of one of the tiny sea creatures – part of the plankton – that practically forms the basis of the food chain in the sea. And this poisoned the larger shellfish, and the small fish, and then the bigger fish . . .'

'But it has been tested.' The Professor's protest sounded feeble, even to her own ears.

'I wish that were true,' Edwin burst out passionately. 'Has it been tested to see what happens when it is left in the sea? Has it? That's what we mean by things being only half done, half guessed at, in your time. I wish I could tell you about how much trouble there's been in the time between you and me.'

'The Age of Amateurs,' the Minister said grimly.

'Yes.'

'But, Edwin, be fair. We do our best, and we make mistakes. With more knowledge, people may make less mistakes, and we do try to put things right. You talk as if everyone in the past were careless or stupid or downright bad. But we aren't. If we were, where would the foundation stones for a better future come from? Who could make the jump from bad to good in one leap? No one! You know that as well as I do. That isn't the way we work – every act leads to the next act, and we are all part of a chain from the past to the future. We make mistakes. We try to put them right. That's what being a human being is all about, at least it seems so to me.'

If it were possible for a telepathic projection to blush, Edwin was blushing now.

'Do forgive me,' he said humbly. 'You are right, of course.' He went on speaking intensely to the Minister.

'When I attacked you in that rude way, it was because of the pain I feel about the poisoned sea. You have not seen it, I have. Every day the beaches are black and stinking from the dead things.' Edwin swallowed, not wanting to go on.

'I told the Minister about the dolphins,' Tim said quickly, 'but he doesn't really know how important they are to you.'

'I'll tell him, then. The story starts about four hundred years ago, when people started using dolphins as sea carriers and messengers, because they could be trained to find "home", like carrier pigeons do in your time. They are loving and intelligent, and learn quickly. Their thinking capacity grew as new demands were made on them, and only the barrier of language kept the dolphins from being true friends and equals.'

'Then, fifty or so years ago, the telepathic microcyb was invented, which made it possible to see into each other's minds. Because the dolphins were wise about the sea, they helped us find new places to grow food, and this teamwork grew until the poison started, about five years ago. Everyone who lives near the sea, as I do, has a pet dolphin. My own pet, Beppo, is living in a tank now, in my garden. He needs the sea and he needs other dolphins. Without them he is going to die . . .'

The Professor got up suddenly. She looked very angry. The story seemed to have affected her deeply – at last.

'Come on, George. Get off your backside and do something!'

The Minister nodded. But he still wanted to ask Edwin something else. 'The Tribaxin, Edwin, do you think your own scientists will find a way to stop the chain reaction spreading?'

'They don't know. They hope so – especially if there isn't too much of it.'

'I promise you, and your Elders, that I will do all I can, all I can,' he repeated, 'but you do realize I can't control what happens in the future. I might be able to stop the dumping of any more Tribaxin – I hope I can. I might be able to prevent any more being made in this country, or at least the scientists might be able to change the formula. But there are so many things . . .' He shook his head sadly.

'One step at a time,' the Professor said softly. 'One thing leads to another, remember, Minister.'

He nodded and smiled at her, a big smile as if he had made a happy decision. He got up from his chair and walked over to a table where the telephone stood.

'Can you stay with us a little while longer?' he asked, as casually as if he were the boy living next door, but his meaning was clear. How long could the Elders use their strength to project Edwin back in time?

'I can stay a little while longer. Everything is all right here. Your words have given the Elders new heart. Also,' he added charmingly, 'they say there is no barrier here to fight against, which would exhaust them. You are all receptive and kind.'

'Thank you,' the Minister said, pleased. 'Now, I won't be a moment.'

He dialled a number and spoke softly for a few minutes. The voice at the other end (was it the Prime Minister?) gave him the necessary permission. He then dialled another number, and spoke in sharper tones to somebody else.

Then he turned to Edwin and smiled. 'There, that's settled. I'll make sure about the stocks being destroyed tomorrow. And we shall do all we can to get international agreement about any dumping in the sea.'

So, with two phone calls, the Minister set in motion the events which he later called 'tying up the loose ends'. He knew it would take weeks and perhaps years to really 'tie up the loose ends'. But Tim, when he told Ellen about it later, made the Minister sound like a hero, a hero who could change history with just two phone calls.

16

The Dolphins

'There,' the Minister said kindly to Edwin, 'your dolphin should be safe now. If only your scientists can contain this phase of the poisoning, there won't be any more.'

A beam of happiness seem to emanate from Edwin. He could not speak, but, of course, they could all feel his relief and hope.

'I'm interested in this use of dolphins,' the Professor mused.

'About time,' Tim thought.

'What a difference these telecybs must make to their brains. How much do you communicate?'

'I know Beppo so well, I already had a good idea what he was feeling, even before he started to wear telecybs. Now, of course, it's practically like speaking. Before he got ill, he could always sense my mood, and when I was miserable, he used to clown about and squeak, and look so funny I just had to laugh.'

'Wonderful, wonderful. And you say they need the company of other dolphins? To stay happy?'

'Yes, they get restless and depressed easily.'

'Something to do with the dancing?' Tim put in.

'What dancing?' asked the Professor.

Edwin tried to explain. 'It's a bit like ballet, The dolphins dance their society. Perhaps the right way of putting it is to say they dance their myths. We think it's been going on since – since dolphins began to live in schools. It was discovered by a . . . oh, I forgot, I mustn't give you the person's name. But the one who discovered the dancing spent nearly all their life, just watching the dolphins, learning what their movements meant.'

Just then, Grandfather woke up with a start. They waited to see how he would react to Edwin, in case it gave him a shock. But he smiled and nodded and told them he had heard every word that Edwin had said, 'and I'm damn pleased to see it wasn't a dream. That means you've really done something about the Tribaxin?' he asked the Minister.

'Yes, it's all fixed.'

'What kind of story do the dolphins dance?' Tim asked.

'Do you know,' Edwin began, 'that whales and dolphins are thought to have come from the land some time millions and millions of years ago? They were probably a kind of grass-eating animal.'

'Like cows?' Tim almost shouted with disbelief.

'That's right. As much like cows as anything. But we can't know for sure. The dolphins seem to have an idea they came from the land, and this story is about how it happened.'

'This person I was telling you about, who studied the dolphins, watched them do the same dance, over and over again. It seemed to be quite an important one, because there were always crowds of them there to watch. It seemed to tell the story of the first dolphins to go into the sea. Sometimes they get so caught up in the dance, they throw themselves up on to the shore.'

'That's not much of a story. It sounds like the person, whoever he is, has just made it up.' This was Grandfather's response.

Edwin tried to explain. 'Do you like music? Do you ever listen to music?'

'Yes,' he nodded hesitatingly. 'Not much, but sometimes I like to.'

'How do you know that what you understand from the music is exactly what the composer meant?'

Tim felt sorry for his Grandfather.

'Does it really matter if what you get out of it and what the composer meant are exactly the same?' he asked.

'No, I suppose it doesn't. That's my point.'

Surprisingly, the Professor seemed to agree with Grandfather. 'I was just going to say the same thing. What you are telling us is not a dolphin story, but a human story, made up by this whoever it is who watches the dolphins swimming about.'

'Do go on,' the Minister begged, trying to unruffle everybody's feelings. 'Of course we have to interpret the story in human terms. After all, the dolphin's world is totally different from our own. And without the use of words, the story must mean something quite different to them. But we understand that, don't we?'

They nodded or grunted in agreement, so Edwin continued with the story.

'I said this dance was supposed to be about the origins of the dolphins. They do this dance all over the world, each school dances it at least twice a year. Sometimes the leaders, who get so exhausted at the end, have to be rescued, when they throw themselves on to the land. And sometimes the other dolphins get underneath them and hold them up.'

Tim felt a thrill of excitement, for he had heard of whales holding each other up when they were ill, or when the females were giving birth. 'But why did the dolphins leave the land in the first place?'

'The dance seems to say that they didn't leave the land – it disappeared beneath them. It rained for a very long time, and the dolphins got hungrier and hungrier as the sea came in more and more, mile by mile. So they changed into animals that could swim in the sea, although they were still mammals and had to breathe air. And the dance is also about how they look for a new land and a time when they can be released from their fishy form,' said Edwin.

Tim felt exhilarated and at the same time a little sad. 'It's a lovely story. Do you know any more?'

'Lots,' Edwin laughed. 'All about humans, and monsters of the deep, and giant squids. But I can't tell you any more.'

And then Tim noticed that Edwin was beginning to fade.

'Oh, no,' he pleaded, close to tears. 'Please don't go yet. Please stay a little bit longer.'

'I have to go, friend,' Edwin said faintly, regretfully. 'The Elders are very tired.'

Tim had forgotten that it was only because of the Elders that Edwin was there with them.

'Edwin, I won't see you ever again.'

The faint form of Edwin shook his head, and tried to smile. Already they could see the sofa through his body.

'I wish you luck, Tim,' he managed to say. 'I am so glad to have met you.'

'And you, Edwin, and you. And I do hope Beppo is going to be all right. Give my love to him, please, will you, Edwin?'

'And all will be well . . .' Edwin was no longer there. Tim looked at the spot where his friend had just been sitting, and a dreadful ache took hold of his throat. It was all over. All the questions he had wanted to ask would never be answered now. He would never know if Beppo got better. He would never see Edwin again.

It was a long, sad silence for them all.

Grandfather gruffly cleared his throat. 'It'll be all right, now, Tim.'

'Well, this is just . . .' Professor Hellebore was lost for words.

Tim opened his mouth to speak, and the words turned into a huge yawn. He quite simply wanted to curl up on the floor next to the Minister's dog, he was so tired.

'Come on, my lad, bed for you. You and your Grandfather must stay here tonight,' the Minister said simply. 'And you, too, Ann. We need to have a talk about all of this tomorrow, don't you agree? I want to keep it out of the press, I need your help.'

He turned to Tim. 'And I'll arrange for one of the Ministry cars to take you back home tomorrow.'

Ann Hellebore was still sitting quietly, looking at the spot on the sofa where Edwin had last been seen. She had slumped down in her chair, and seemed to be in a state of shock. She even shook herself as if trying to focus on them all.

'You know, that story about the dolphins was quite fascinating. And creepy, too.'

'Creepy? Not creepy, surely,' the Minister said.

'I mean, it's credible. That's what makes it creepy, and its similar to our own myth.'

They were leaving the study now, but Grandfather stopped and looked at the Professor. 'I don't understand what you are on about.'

'What myth?' Tim asked.

'Why, haven't you ever heard of the country that disappeared under the sea "between big lands". It was like Edwin said. Haven't you ever heard of Atlantis?'

She got up and joined them, and put a friendly arm round Tim's shoulder, 'No? Then I'll tell you about it,' she said, as they slowly walked up the stairs.

A Selected List of Fiction from Mammoth

While every effort is made to keep prices low, it is sometimes necessary to increase prices at short notice. Mammoth Books reserves the right to show new retail prices on covers which may differ from those previously advertised in the text or elsewhere.

The prices shown below were correct at the time of going to press.

☐	416 13972 8	**Why the Whales Came**	Michael Morpurgo	£2.50
☐	7497 0034 3	**My Friend Walter**	Michael Morpurgo	£2.50
☐	7497 0035 1	**The Animals of Farthing Wood**	Colin Dann	£2.99
☐	7497 0136 6	**I Am David**	Anne Holm	£2.50
☐	7497 0139 0	**Snow Spider**	Jenny Nimmo	£2.50
☐	7497 0140 4	**Emlyn's Moon**	Jenny Nimmo	£2.25
☐	7497 0344 X	**The Haunting**	Margaret Mahy	£2.25
☐	416 96850 3	**Catalogue of the Universe**	Margaret Mahy	£1.95
☐	7497 0051 3	**My Friend Flicka**	Mary O'Hara	£2.99
☐	7497 0079 3	**Thunderhead**	Mary O'Hara	£2.99
☐	7497 0219 2	**Green Grass of Wyoming**	Mary O'Hara	£2.99
☐	416 13722 9	**Rival Games**	Michael Hardcastle	£1.99
☐	416 13212 X	**Mascot**	Michael Hardcastle	£1.99
☐	7497 0126 9	**Half a Team**	Michael Hardcastle	£1.99
☐	416 08812 0	**The Whipping Boy**	Sid Fleischman	£1.99
☐	7497 0033 5	**The Lives of Christopher Chant**	Diana Wynne-Jones	£2.50
☐	7497 0164 1	**A Visit to Folly Castle**	Nina Beachcroft	£2.25

All these books are available at your bookshop or newsagent, or can be ordered direct from the publisher. Just tick the titles you want and fill in the form below.

Mandarin Paperbacks, Cash Sales Department, PO Box 11, Falmouth, Cornwall TR10 9EN.

Please send cheque or postal order, no currency, for purchase price quoted and allow the following for postage and packing:

UK   80p for the first book, 20p for each additional book ordered to a maximum charge of £2.00.

BFPO   80p for the first book, 20p for each additional book.

Overseas   £1.50 for the first book, £1.00 for the second and 30p for each additional book
including Eire   thereafter.

NAME (Block letters) ....

ADDRESS ....

....

....